MW01286332

A HANDBOOK FOR THE PRODUCTIVE WRITER

33 WAYS YOU CAN FINISH WHAT YOU STARTED

BRYAN COLLINS

Become a Writer Today
http://www.becomeawritertoday.com

A Handbook for the Productive Writer
33 Ways You Can Finish What You Started

Third Edition

By Bryan Collins

www.becomeawritertoday.com

For A.

GET YOUR EXCLUSIVE FREE BONUS

Before you start reading, I've got a great bonus for you.

I have created a **FREE email course** so you can discover how to become more productive and creative.

To get your free email course, please visit becomeawritertoday.com/join and join the Insider List.

CONTENTS

INTRODUCTION

FINISHING A BOOK is tough.

Perhaps you find it difficult to take an idea from conception to completion?

Do you struggle to produce anything meaningful from a few hours of writing each week?

Or maybe you make a habit of beginning and then abandoning blog posts, articles and stories?

Take a deep breath. It's OK.

We've all been there.

Writing is hard work. You've got to think of an idea, shape it into something usable, write it, rewrite, edit, and then rewrite some more. It's a mentally and physically demanding job, and many writers give up before they reach the end.

If you picked up this book, you're a different kind of writer. You're the kind of writer who doesn't give up on troublesome writing projects. You're the kind of writer who is always looking for ways to improve. You're also the kind of writer who wants to finish what you started.

Whether you are working on a blog post, article, academic paper, short story or even a novel; if you're passionate about your topic (hopefully you are) and you're prepared to put the work in, you will reach the end.

I'm certain any aspiring writer can learn how to finish their work. It doesn't take a genius, a divine gift or the discipline of a Zen monk to finish a writing project.

Don't be intimidated by the process of writing or by the idea of becoming a more productive writer. You can cultivate your ability to write and to finish what you started by showing up in front of the blank page and working at it every day.

I've spent years working as a journalist, copywriter and blogger, I've made a lot of mistakes, some of which were public and some of which were private, and I've learnt many hard lessons about writing, productivity, and creativity.

I've studied popular productivity methods at length and written about them extensively for my blog Become a Writer Today. I've also spent time reading hundreds of articles and books about the art of writing.

It's a subject I'm passionate about.

In this book, I'm going to share this passion with you through 33 simple but effective productivity strategies, which any writer can use to write every day and finish what they started.

What You'll Discover in This Handbook

In this practical book, you will discover 33 simple but effective productivity and writing strategies. To help you get out of your creative jams, I've included various proven writing and creative prompts that you can use today to kick-start your troublesome writing projects. This book isn't specifically about fiction or non-fiction writing, but I do make references to both types of writing.

My hope for you is that through using this book, you will become a more confident and professional writer who ships on time. Using these 33 strategies, you'll be able to write every day, create a writing habit that sticks and finish what you started.

You will become the productive writer.

How to Use This Handbook

Why 33 productivity strategies?

I started *A Handbook for the Productive Writer* by writing 101 writing strategies. I formulated these 101 strategies by studying how literary heavyweights and renowned non-fiction writers approach their craft. I also spent time studying the methodology behind popular productivity techniques that business people use to accomplish more in their personal and professional lives.

My intention was to find that point where business and the arts intersect, and in this book I make regular references to the authors that you and I can learn from.

I'm not going to lie to you.

Writing 101 strategies was hard work, and I almost gave up writing this book (twice), but writing 101 strategies made the job of writing 33 strategies feel achievable.

Think of the marathon runner who has to run 26 miles: the first 13 are easy; it's the second 13 that present the real problems.

So once I had 101 strategies, I took Ernest Hemingway's advice.

He said, "The first draft of everything is shit."

Authors like Hemingway can teach the rest of us how to achieve anything with words, ideas, and a blank page.

I worked through each of my 101 strategies, and I discarded what wasn't working. This kind of brutal editing is a process every productive writer becomes intimately familiar with.

Then, I refined my research and ideas into 33 essential strategies that will help you get to the end of whatever you're writing.

What I've just described—the strategy of generating more ideas by setting the bar higher—is just one of the 33 strategies that you will discover in this book.

You can use the 33 strategies in this book to write a blog post, a newsletter, an article, a college assignment, a short story, a book, or even a novel.

I wrote each of these 33 strategies as standalone chapters with actionable steps that you can take today. Although there is a natural order to this book, you can dip in and out of each strategy and apply it to your current writing project.

You can read this book from start to finish, you can use it as a companion guide, or you can apply the individual strategies that are most relevant for how you like to work or write.

Let's get started.

1

LEAVE YOUR INTRODUCTION TILL LAST

LET ME TELL you a secret.

Productive writers create their introduction last.

The purpose of the first sentence is to convince a reader to read the second sentence. The purpose of the first paragraph is to convince the reader to read the second. The purpose of the first chapter… and so on.

Think about it: what's the first thing a customer in a bookshop looks at when they open a new book? Unless you're one of those crazy types who likes to read the ending, it's the first line.

Almost every writer I've met writes their first paragraph and their first sentence last.

It doesn't matter if you're writing a book, an article, a blog post or copy for a webpage—you must capture and hold the reader's attention. And the reader's attention is a valuable commodity.

Writing a solid first line or a good opening is hard work. If you don't know what the subsequent sentences, paragraphs, and chapters are about, writing a great opening is impossible.

During your next writing project, don't worry about the beginning until you reach the end. Then, read through your work and summarise it in a sentence or two. If you can come up with a good hook or metaphor to draw the reader in, even better. Once you're happy with your introduction, re-read your conclusion and explore how you can link the two together. Perhaps there's an idea or a metaphor that you can return to? Or maybe you can use similar language to answer a question you raised in your introduction?

Your introduction and conclusion should be like two poles on a magnetic field; their purpose is to hold your work together and give it consistency.

Whatever your approach, work hard on your opening and even harder on your first line. Smooth it, buff it, polish it and make it shine. When the reader reads your opening line, they should find it irresistible.

Your first line can and should make the reader feel angry, inspired, curious, motivated, lonely, hungry, sad, happy or thirsty for your next line. Whatever you do, don't bore them with a long, ponderous sentence. Make your reader feel something, and they'll keep reading.

Whenever I'm struggling to find an opening for something I'm writing, I go back and read great first lines for inspiration. With this in mind, here are ten of the greatest first lines of all time. Each of these first lines succeeds because they make the reader feel something.

These great first lines compel us to read on and find out what happens next:

- "Call me Ishmael." – Herman Melville, *Moby-Dick* (1851)

- "It was a bright cold day in April, and the clocks were striking thirteen." – George Orwell, *1984* (1949)

- "It was the best of times, it was the worst of times, it was the age of wisdom, it was the age of foolishness, it was the epoch of belief, it was the epoch of incredulity, it was the season of Light, it was the season of Darkness, it was the spring of hope, it was the winter of despair." – Charles Dickens, *A Tale of Two Cities* (1859)

- "Lolita, light of my life, fire of my loins." – Vladimir Nabokov, *Lolita* (1955)

- "Happy families are all alike; every unhappy family is unhappy in its own way." – Leo Tolstoy, *Anna Karenina* (1877)

- "It is a truth universally acknowledged, that a single man in possession of a good fortune, must be in want of a wife." – Jane Austen, *Pride and Prejudice* (1813)

- "It was a queer, sultry summer, the summer they electrocuted the Rosenbergs, and I didn't know what I was doing in New York." – Sylvia Plath, *The Bell Jar* (1963)

- "If you really want to hear about it, the first thing you'll probably want to know is where I was born, and what my lousy childhood was like, and how my parents were occupied and all before they had me, and all that David Copperfield kind of crap, but I don't feel like going into it, if you want to know the truth." – J.D Salinger, *The Catcher In The Rye* (1951)

- "In my younger and more vulnerable years my father gave me some advice that I've been turning over in my mind ever since. Whenever you feel like criticising anyone, he told me, just remember that all the people in this world haven't had the advantages that you've had." – F. Scott Fitzgerald, *The Great Gatsby* (1925)

- "As Gregor Samsa awoke one morning from uneasy dreams he found himself transformed in his bed into a monstrous vermin." – Franz Kafka, *The Metamorphosis* (1915)

How to Use the Inverted Pyramid

Journalists use the inverted pyramid to arrange the key facts of what they are writing.

This concept came about because the editors and printers of early newspapers sometimes didn't have enough print space to fit stories into their papers. They needed a way of removing information quickly to make the text of each story fit, and cutting off the bottom paragraphs of news stories was the fastest way to do this.

So journalists started writing the most important point first, the second most important point second, and so on. Even though printing technology has improved, the inverted pyramid still applies because newspaper readers don't always read a story all the way through. A reader will glance at a headline and if it's of interest they'll pick the paper up and read the rest of the story.

Today, journalists use the headline, the first sentence, and the first paragraph to answer the following questions in increasing levels of detail:

- What happened?
- To whom did it happen?

- Where did it happen?
- Why did it happen?
- How did it happen?
- When did it happen?

Writers also use the inverted pyramid for web pages because the average visitor doesn't stay for more than 10 to 20 seconds on a webpage. So, an online writer has to capture the reader's attention by putting the most important information first and by writing for people who scan digital copy.

The inverted pyramid works for short, non-fiction writing projects. You can apply it to newsletters, social media posts, copy for webpages, blog posts, or articles. If you are writing for the web, you can use the inverted pyramid to get to the point faster. Make it your job to say what is most important first, make your text scannable and get the reader to stay a little longer.

The inverted pyramid isn't as effective when your writing has more room to breathe, and when you can count on the reader's attention (e.g. in a thesis or 3,000-plus word feature article) because you have the time and space to expand on your arguments or tell a story.

Opening with Flair

The introduction is the hardest part of any article or story to write. If you're struggling to create a compelling opening, leave it till last. When you're done, you'll have a better idea of how to begin.

If you're still stuck, open like a journalist. They write their articles with the end in mind. They know what their news story is about, and they know what they are saying before they start writing. A journalist doesn't begin a news article hoping that by the time they reach the last paragraph they will have said something important or newsworthy.

Neither does the productive writer.

The Inverted Pyramid

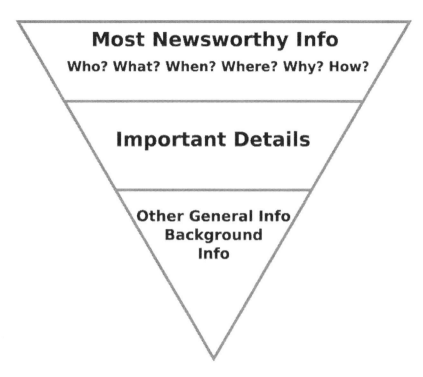

The Inverted Pyramid, via Wikimedia and The Air Force Departmental Publishing Office (AFDPO, 2011)

2

WARM UP LIKE A PRO

"If you want to be the best, you have to do things that other people aren't willing to do." – Michael Phelps

Do you warm up before you write?

The Olympic swimmer Michael Phelps swims in a separate pool to the competition pool for 45 minutes before a big race. The world's fastest man, Usain Bolt, practices sprinting near the track before he competes. And tennis champion Roger Federer skips, jumps and stretches before a match.

Writers who want to become more productive should apply the same approach to their craft.

It takes 5 or 10 minutes of writing to forget the distractions of the day, warm up and pay attention to whatever you're supposed to be working on. These first few minutes of writing may not produce anything of merit.

The purpose of the first few minutes of any writing session is to adjust your mind towards the task of writing. Warming up will help you overcome procrastination, and if you do it regularly, it will make those first few minutes of writing less painful.

There are lots of ways you can warm up before you write.

Reading poetry or listening to music can fire up the left side of your brain for more creative work. Reading a passage of a book or an article can engage your critical faculties for non-fiction writing. Printing out, reading and annotating the entirety of the previous day's work is also useful if you're about to embark on an editing session.

Alternatively, you can use a writing prompt to warm up today.

101 Writing Prompts To Jumpstart Your Writing Today

These writing prompts aren't meant as final first lines for your work.

Instead, you can use them as a jumping off point into your work or for free writing.

Take one of these lines, write it down and then free write whatever else comes to mind.

Do this for at least 30 minutes.

This is long enough to accomplish something on the blank page but not so long that it feels overwhelming.

Later when you've written something more polished, go back and delete the writing prompt.

Alternatively, if you dislike my selection of prompts, take a great first line from your favourite book, poem or story and use that.

Whatever your choice, writing prompts will help you stand on the shoulders of giants. And up there, you can see for miles.

1. "I remember the last time I…"
2. "I remember the first time I…"
3. "The next time I…"
4. "It tasted like…"
5. "It felt like…"
6. "It sounded like…"
7. "We were wrong about…"
8. "We were right about…"
9. "That was the day we…"
10. "This is our new…"
11. "It's here."
12. "I learnt that…"
13. "I made a terrible mistake when…"
14. "Nobody expected us to…"
15. "Do you know why…"
16. "It's always important to…"

17. "Most people don't know this but…"
18. "I probably shouldn't be telling you this but…"
19. "Here's a secret nobody knows…"
20. "I do this because…"
21. "Admit it."
22. "I found out that…"
23. "He gave us a…"
24. "She took a…"
25. "We found a…"
26. "I was in pain."
27. "We discovered…"
28. "Today is a good day for…"
29. "Tomorrow is a bad day for…"
30. "This time it will be different."
31. "We need to talk about…"
32. "You need to face up to…"
33. "Our only hope is…"
34. "On my desk I can see…"
35. "Outside the window there's…"
36. "I ate…"
37. "If I was…"
38. "When I'm…"
39. "Go to…"
40. "Now that we…"
41. "We argued about…"
42. "Being wrong is hard because…"
43. "Being right is lonely because…"
44. "Together we can…."
45. "Apart we are…"
46. "Let me guess."
47. "If I understand you correctly, you think…"
48. "My friend is…"
49. "I love her because…"
50. "I hate him because…"
51. "We're going to…"
52. "Let's take a trip to…"
53. "My favourite…"

54. "I'm lost."
55. "We want to get to…"
56. "The weather is…"
57. "We're going to eat…"
58. "Food is…"
59. "Water is…"
60. "Money is…"
61. "Help is…"
62. "Sex is…"
63. "Last night I dreamt of…"
64. "I slept for…"
65. "I'm working for…"
66. "I failed at…"
67. "I succeeded at…"
68. "You showed me how to…"
69. "He explained that…"
70. "She made us laugh when…"
71. "My hero is…"
72. "My enemy is…"
73. "I regret…"
74. "This time we went too far."
75. "I told him…"
76. "She told me…"
77. "I looked in the mirror and saw…."
78. "Black."
79. "White."
80. "I awoke at 3 am and realised…"
81. "I should have listened."
82. "He won't do that again."
83. "It was the first storm of the year…"
84. "Her eyes are…"
85. "His hands make me want to…"
86. "She tastes like…"
87. "He feels like…"
88. "Danger."
89. "How can we…"
90. "Open your…"

91. "Keep it safe."
92. "It's a new day."
93. "It's later than we think."
94. "If I ever see another…"
95. "The best day of my life was…"
96. "The worst day of my life was…"
97. "When I'm king…"
98. "You could be a queen of…"
99. "Looking back…"
100. "They caught me."
101. "I was crushed because…"

How Free Writing Can Help You

Free writing is a simple skill to learn, and it's one every productive writer should have in their toolbox.

To free write, all you have to do is sit at your desk and write about anything that comes to mind without interruption for 5, 10 or 20 minutes. Even if you write nothing but gibberish, whatever you do, don't stop writing.

When you free write, you're not trying to accomplish or complete anything on the blank page.

The author Mark Levy is an expert on free writing, and he says in his book, *Accidental Genius*, "Free writing…pushes the brain to think longer, deeper, and more unconventionally than it normally would."

He's right.

Free writing also offers a number of other benefits to writers. It can help you clear mental blocks, come up with new and better ideas, write more honestly, think differently from your peers, and even find a new perspective for your writing projects.

You can free write a cover letter for a job application, copy for your website, a blog post, a magazine article or even a chapter for your book.

If you want to try free writing as a warm-up exercise for your current writing project, don't worry about capturing fully formed ideas.

Instead, just type or write about anything that comes to mind when you think about your current writing project. It's OK if you jump from one idea to the next. Document your thoughts as they arise without holding back. Don't edit or censure yourself. Even if something daft comes, like the sound of a dog on the street, write that down too. And if someone interrupts your train of thought, record that you were interrupted.

If you keep free writing, you will overtake your brain's ability to edit and break past your internal critic. You will reach a place where you can write about wild ideas and make connections that otherwise wouldn't have been possible if you'd held back.

Your word count will shoot up and even if most of what you write is rubbish, at the end of your free writing session, you can extract one or two good ideas and then spend time developing these into something more usable for your current writing project.

Practical Free Writing Tips

Write Without Editing Yourself

Free writing only works if you don't question or criticise every sentence, idea and story that you put down on the blank page. Instead, let the words flow freely from your fingers onto the page without pausing or questioning what you are saying.

Then, when you've finished your free writing for the day, spend time polishing, buffing and making your prose shine.

Write Whatever Comes to Mind

Free writing enables you to follow a train of thought in new and exciting directions. Some of these directions may be dead ends, but they're still worth exploring.

When you're free writing, record what you're thinking or if you feel distracted—it doesn't matter if it's unrelated to the topic you're writing about. This could mean recording the sound of a dog on the street, the colour of a plant on your desk, or even a swear word.

Don't hold back.

Time Your Free Writing Sessions

Get a clock (or the timer on your computer), set it for 25 minutes and write. Then, when the buzzer sounds, take a short break and repeat. Do this two to four times before taking a longer break.

Free Write for an Hour or Longer

This is a tough tip for writers to implement.

If you're struggling to make a breakthrough, free write for an extended period without taking a break. Your job is to keep going until you make a breakthrough.

Yes, this is mentally and physically demanding but you don't have to do it very often, and it will help you break through those difficult barriers every writer faces at some point.

Keep Your Hand Moving

This tip is straight from the pages of Natalie Goldberg's excellent book *Writing Down the Bones: Freeing the Writer Within.*

An advocate of free writing, or writing practice as she calls it, Natalie recommends "keeping your hand moving."

If you're a typist, don't take your fingers from the keys until you've finished writing. If you prefer a pen, this means keeping the pen pressed between your fingers. And if you like to dictate your writing, keep the dictaphone recording until you're done.

Keep a List of Topics to Free Write About

I use Evernote to organise my writing. Inside Evernote, I keep a notebook full of topics that I want to free write about. Examples include ideas for short stories, sentence fragments, blog posts and ideas that I want to expand on.

Then when I want to free write, I pick one item from my notebook and go with it. Keeping these types of lists means I spend less time looking for a topic and more time free writing.

Combine Free Writing with Other Types of Writing

Free writing is just one writing technique you can employ to advance your work.

There are times when it makes more sense to plan your writing in advance or aim towards a target word count. Combining free writing with other types of writing sessions will help you mix things up during the week, test your boundaries, and avoid becoming bored with the process.

Keep Your Cast-offs

Free writing produces a lot of leftover ideas that don't immediately belong anywhere. Don't throw this writing in the bin or delete it. Instead, keep your cast-offs in your journal or in a file on your computer. There will come a time when it makes sense to return to these leftovers and extract something useful. And even if this time never comes, these leftovers serve as markers for your progress as a writer.

Read a Book in Your Niche, Take an Idea and Expand

I read a lot of non-fiction books. This means I regularly come across ideas that surprise me, inspire me or confound me. Sometimes, I take these ideas and expand on them during free writing sessions. Free writing about ideas helps me internalise them and figure out how I can apply them to my creative life.

If you want to do the same, underline key passages in the books you are reading, write notes in the margins, and review these notes when you've finished with the book (the Kindle is ideal for this). Then, pick one or two ideas and use these as topics for your next free writing sessions.

Free Write a Problem Upside Down

Are you having trouble with a particularly difficult writing project? Perhaps the feedback from a client wasn't helpful? Or maybe you can't figure out the right arc for your story?

Write down this problem at the top of your page.

Now, free write everything about the problem that's bothering you and even what you're afraid of. Then, free write all the solutions you can think of.

It doesn't matter how preposterous, outlandish or impractical they sound. If you get lucky, you'll make a breakthrough and even if you don't, you are still venting your frustrations and practice writing at the same time.

Think of it as therapy and writing practice rolled into one.

Why You Should Free Write For Kicks

As a writer, there are times when you need to reach your goals, hit a word count and press publish. There are other times when writing is supposed to be fun, when you need to try something different or when you must go in a new direction.

For these other times, free writing is the perfect writing technique. This week, allocate 30 minutes of time for free writing. Use it to free write about whatever you want. Think of it as your guilty pleasure.

Are you still unsure about free writing? Why not free write about the ways it can help you finish what you started? Who knows where you'll end up?

3

STOP WAITING FOR INSPIRATION (IT'S NOT COMING)

"Don't be daunted. Just do your job. Continue to show up for your piece of it, whatever that might be." – Elizabeth Gilbert

WHAT WOULD HAPPEN if a professional athlete stopped training for an event because they were tired of their sport?

If he or she made a habit of not training, they'd lose their next event.

What would happen if an engineer stopped working on a construction project because he didn't feel excited about plans for the project?

He'd lose his job.

What happens to the writer who waits for inspiration to arrive?

She doesn't write at all.

Writing is hard work. It's demanding and time-consuming, and it requires you to sit in one place and concentrate for extended periods of time. If you want to write professionally, treat it seriously. Like any profession, it's your job to turn up in front of the blank page each day and not just when inspiration arrives. It's your duty to write even when you don't feel like writing, when you're tired, angry, anxious or afraid.

Leave divine moments of inspiration for the creative geniuses.

The American short story writer and author John Updike wasn't one for waiting around for inspiration. He wrote for several hours each day. Updike published his first work—a collection of poetry—*The Carpentered Hen* in 1958. Thereafter, he published a book almost every year.

"I've never believed that one should wait until one is inspired, because I think that the pleasures of not writing are so great that if you ever start indulging them, you'll never write again," he said.

Stop waiting around for an idea or solution to whatever you're having problems with. Force yourself into the chair and start to write. The first few sentences may not make much sense but, several sentences in, you'll realise you're not as tired or devoid of ideas as you thought; you were just procrastinating.

Even if you turn up and produce nothing of value, at least you put in a morning or an evening's work. Like Elizabeth Gilbert mentioned in her 2009 TED talk, if you keep turning up, you will wear your writer's block down.

The Beast Wants What it Wants

The subconscious is a powerful beast.

And it needs food and attention.

Take notes, turn up every day in front of the blank page and make a concerted effort to finish what you're working on. The writer who does this understands how important it is to feed his or her inner beast.

If you write sales copy, your subconscious is hungry for the words that sell, for words written by talented copywriters.

If you write articles for magazines, your subconscious is waiting for exotic, fresh, and colourful stories.

If you write blog posts, it wants to devour in-depth, meaningful posts so it can present you with new ideas.

If you write fiction, your subconscious craves anecdotes, stories, characters and dialogue.

Keeping the beast happy also means giving it time and space to roam free through your mind.

I'm talking about day-dreaming.

Most creative people are familiar with those small eureka moments of life whereby a solution suddenly presents itself when you're working on something else entirely. These ideas can turn up when you're in the shower, eating a meal, watching television, out for a walk or even on the toilet. Of course, it would be more convenient if we could summon these ideas at will in front of the blank page, but the subconscious is a wild animal; it can't be tamed.

The French artist Henri Matisse gave his subconscious time and space while painting landscapes. He sometimes stopped working to meditate on the environment around him. He did this at length before returning to his canvas with a new perspective.

Matisse did pretty well for himself in the end. As one of the greatest and most productive painters of the twentieth century, he finished several dozen masterpieces during his lifetime. So, don't be afraid to pause what you are doing.

Let the beast run free.

Get to Work, Just Like Einstein

Are you still procrastinating?

Do you need just a little bit more encouragement to pick up the pen?

Are you still thinking, "but I could accomplish more if I didn't have to do all these other things?"

Take some productivity lessons from Albert Einstein.

Albert Einstein is one of the most famous scientific writers of all time (and a personal hero). Although he is more famous for his mathematical equations than his writing, Einstein's life shows we writers can succeed because of the day-to-day struggles of life and not in spite of them.

Einstein's Peers Repeatedly Rejected Him

During his early twenties, Einstein spent several years seeking employment as a teaching assistant. He struggled to find meaningful work, and he found it difficult to get his dissertation published as part of his application for a doctorate. Einstein even sent professors copies of his dissertation with a postage-paid card, to encourage them to reply and offer feedback (sometimes we take email for granted!).

Numerous leading professors and employers in Germany, Austria, Italy and Switzerland rejected Einstein repeatedly. At one stage, Einstein became so despondent about his career that he contemplated abandoning science for engineering.

His father, an engineer, even wrote to Wilhelm Ostwald, the Professor of Chemistry of Leipzig, and implored Ostwald to read Albert's paper and write a few words of encouragement.

Ostwald didn't reply (although much later he did nominate Einstein for the Nobel Prize).

Even later, after Einstein published a series of landmark papers that overturned the basics of physics, it took him several more years to achieve the academic and professional recognition he deserved.

Today, writers have much more opportunities than Einstein to make their voices heard. If a gatekeeper refuses our work, we can use a blog to build a platform; we can enter contests, or we can self-publish. Today, it doesn't take a genius to find an audience.

Einstein Found Success on the Outside

After a long period of searching for employment, Einstein found a job working in a Swiss patent office in Bern, in 1902.

There, he worked eight hours a day, for five and six days a week for six years. In his spare time, Einstein conducted his research and wrote. In 1905, the third-class patent examiner published four momentous scientific papers, one of that formed the basis for the most famous scientific equation of all time: $E=mc2$. Even then, it took Einstein several more years to achieve an academic posting in a university.

Einstein's life shows us it's possible to succeed in the face of competing personal and professional demands. There's nothing stopping an aspiring writer holding down a full-time job during the day and pursuing their passion at night.

Einstein Pursued Multiple Interests

Einstein loved music since he was a child, and he became an accomplished violin player. He often entertained dinner party guests, academics, friends and his family by playing Mozart.

He didn't care much for material possessions or appearances, but he did bring his violin almost everywhere. Einstein once played with the noted Russian violinist Toscha Seidel, and afterwards explained his theory of relativity to Seidel.

He only stopped playing later in life when it became too hard for his fingers to use the violin.

Einstein's first love was science, but he still made time for other passions and interests. Writers don't have to pursue their craft at all costs; if anything, your writing will improve if you make time for other passions.

Einstein Challenged Himself and Others

Einstein saw himself as a non-conformist and a rebel. This belief system was a result of the times he lived in and his personal character.

Einstein lived through two World Wars, and he had to leave Hitler's Germany for America because he was Jewish. As a younger man, he suggested academic life wasn't conducive to great work, and according to his biographer Walter Isaacson, he took delight in challenging the prevailing wisdom of his academic peers.

From the 1920s onwards, many of Einstein's theories were challenged or overturned by a new branch of physics: quantum mechanics. This branch of physics described randomness in nature, but Einstein dismissed it saying, "God does not play dice."

He spent the later part of his life researching a unified theory that could unify his general theory of relativism with electromagnetism.

Einstein's contemporaries, who were more concerned with quantum mechanics, regarded his quest as rather quaint and even as a waste of Einstein's time.

Einstein didn't care.

Always the rebel, he felt he'd achieved enough status and security in life to spend time researching areas of physics that his younger peers would have been discredited for spending time on.

For Einstein, pursuing a passion was more important than what others thought of him or how he spent his time.

It matters less how much success a writer enjoys; what matters more is challenging ourselves, publishing our work, and avoiding complacency.

Einstein Didn't Regard His Craft as Work

In 1955, a 76-year-old Einstein died in hospital from a longstanding stomach ailment.

On his death bed, he left twelve sets of equations which formed parts of Einstein's search for a unified field theory. He also left an undelivered speech, which he had just written for Israel Independence day.

I'm not suggesting writing on your death bed, but Einstein's story demonstrates a life's work can take on a greater meaning if we're passionate enough about our craft.

At the very least, remember Einstein's advice for scientists and by extension writers: "If you can't explain it simply, you don't understand it well enough."

Failing like a Genius

Genius or not, Einstein had lots of personal flaws. Albert married Marić Mileva in 1903, and he divorced her in 1919 after a difficult and unhappy marriage. He also rarely saw his son Eduard Tete, who had schizophrenia and had a more difficult life in various mental health institutions.

Einstein married his second wife Elsa Löwenthal in 1919 and, although they were married until her death in 1936, he had several affairs with other women.

After her death, Einstein praised a friend for managing to live in harmony with a woman, saying this was one thing he failed at. He could also be cold and distant and, as a younger man, he often made life harder for himself by deliberately antagonising and challenging his peers.

Einstein succeeded in so many ways in his life, but he also failed and failed often, and he experienced the same pain and suffering many of us go through.

4

IDEAS ARE LIKE FUEL; DON'T RUN OUT

"The knowledge of all things is possible." – Leonardo da Vinci

You can't drive a car without fuel, and you can't write if you haven't got any ideas.

The good news is that unlike fuel, ideas are everywhere. All you have to do is get into the habit of regularly filling up your creative tank, and you will always have fuel for writing. This habit is one accomplished writers, artists and even inventors cultivate.

When Leonardo da Vinci died in 1519, he left behind dozens of notebooks filled with ideas for new art projects, paintings and inventions. Some of these ideas, such as his initial concept for the helicopter, informed future inventions. Da Vinci's journals and notebooks are a triumph of creativity and a reminder of the importance of generating ideas every day. His ideas showed us how we can better understand the world around us.

The academic and scholar Michael Gelb studied da Vinci's notebooks and his life. Gelb recommends anyone who wants to become creative like da Vinci should make a habit of recording new ideas every day.

Gelb writes:

"Busy lives and job responsibilities tend to drive us toward hard conclusions and measurable results, but the exploratory, free-flowing, unfinished, non-judgmental practice of keeping a da Vincian notebook encourages freedom of thought and expansion of perspective. In the manner of the maestro, don't worry about order and logical flow, just record."

Raising the Bar

Get a pen and paper and write down ten or even 100 ideas for whatever you're working on.

Don't judge, dismiss or censor whatever comes to mind. Instead, record your idea and progress quickly to the next one. The task of generating so many new ideas will force your brain to make new connections and mash up old ideas.

If you're struggling to come up with ideas, try writing down at least:

- Ten reasons why something will work/won't work
- Ten reasons why you're for/against something
- Ten ideas you can combine
- Ten things you need to do next
- Ten interviewees you could source
- Ten headlines
- Ten ways to open or close your story with a bang
- Ten questions you need answers to
- Ten unusual facts or pieces of information you possess
- Ten strengths/weaknesses of your chosen topic

Much like free writing, it doesn't matter where your ideas come from, if they're silly or even useless. Aim for quantity over quality. It's easier to generate 100 ideas of variable quality than it is to think of one perfect idea.

After you've captured 35 bad ideas, there's a much higher chance of coming up with one great idea. Conversely, if you try to come up with one great idea for your writing project, it will feel impossible. Raise the bar impossibly high and you will surprise yourself with what you can achieve. At the very least, the more ideas you have to write about, the easier it will be to sit down in front of the blank page.

Every day, I write down ten ideas for blog posts, articles, short stories or even book chapters in my notebook. Some of my ideas are terrible, and others never make it beyond my notebook. However, by the end of the week I have lots of new ideas that I can sift through, and at least one always holds some value.

If I sound borderline obsessive about generating new ideas each day, it's because I don't want to run out of fuel when the time comes to write.

Review What You're Writing About

Once you get into the habit of generating new ideas, you'll find there are too many to act on. There just aren't enough hours in the day and life carries too many commitments for you to write about everything you want.

Here's the thing:

Acting on an idea carries an opportunity cost. When you write about one idea, you're spending time that could be spent writing about something else.

For example, if I've got an idea for a blog post and an idea for a book chapter, I can only do one of these things first. The question is: *how do I decide which is more important?*

Ask yourself why you want to act on an idea and if it's something you're passionate about.

For a long time, I wrote about the wrong ideas. I reviewed products, games, services and music for various Irish newspapers. These articles were easy to write, I got to keep what I reviewed, and I enjoyed the process, at first.

Later though, I recognised I was criticising ideas other people had created and worked on, and it's almost always easier to criticise than it is to create. So I told my editor I didn't want to reviews games, films or music albums anymore. I wanted to concentrate on writing news stories and feature articles. At least this type of writing would give me room to come up with ideas and make better mistakes.

I'm not a journalist anymore and I only review products on my blog if I'm passionate about the product or service and it can help writers accomplish more. I prefer spending my time writing longer, more involved articles that force me to challenge myself, like this book.

This pursuit is harder and more time-consuming, but it's also more satisfying.

Becoming a more productive writer means coming up with ideas every day and then spending time refining your ideas down to an essential few. Archive or discard what you don't need and then use the best ones as fuel for the blank page.

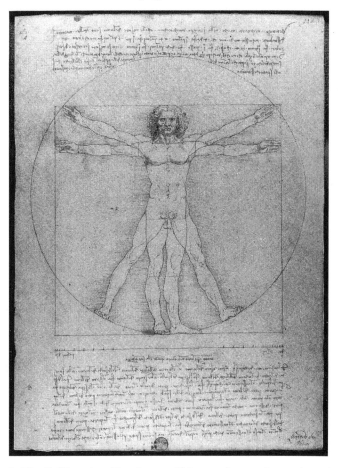

Leonardo da Vinci's Vitruvian Man is one of his most famous journal entries, via Luc Viatour / www.Lucnix.be (2007)

BUILD A PERSONAL LIBRARY (AND USE IT)

"…we judge it is of great service in studies. . . to bestow diligence and labor in setting down common-places; as it affords matter to invention, and collects and strengthens the judgment." – Francis Bacon

PRODUCTIVE WRITERS KEEP a personal library where they store their best ideas, what they've learnt, information about what they've read, and even notes on what they'd like to write next. I'm not referring to building a spare room in your house that you fill with shelves and books.

Instead, you can create your personal library by keeping a commonplace book and a swipe file. You can also keep one by annotating your favourite books and articles, and by writing your ideas down.

How to Keep a Commonplace Book

A commonplace book will help you marshal research for your writing projects. Before the modern age, commonplace books were popular. They were a sort of personal, pre-internet repository of letters, medical information, quotes, facts, experiences, anecdotes and personal histories. They were also a way for individuals, families and communities to sort and store knowledge about their lives.

Historical figures, authors and poets such as Marcus Aurelius, Napoleon, Thomas Jefferson, Francis Bacon, John Milton and W.H. Auden all kept or published commonplace books.

More recently, the American author Ryan Holiday explained how he uses a commonplace book to write his books.

He said, "The purpose of the [commonplace] book is to record and organise these gems for later use in your life, in your business, in your writing, speaking or whatever it is that you do."

A commonplace book will help you become a more productive writer because when the time comes to write your next book or article, you will already have a resource of relevant information that you can draw on. You will be the kind of writer who is always researching, learning and on the hunt for new ideas.

You won't need to spend hours researching because you will already know what you want to write about. Your research will form part of your creative life.

A commonplace book only works if you read widely and mark what's relevant as you go. Then later, you should extract useful information and put it in your commonplace book. You can use a paper-based or digital system to store this information in your commonplace book.

Whatever your preference, categorise entries in your commonplace book with terms that apply to your work and your life.

For example, I use the term 'blog' for ideas and articles that are relevant to blog posts I want to write. I use the term 'journal' to record ideas and information for entries in my journal. When I was writing this book, I categorised various entries in my commonplace book by terms related to each strategy in this book.

To get value from your commonplace book, make a habit of regularly reviewing and reorganising your entries. This way, the wisdom you're gathering will sink into each of your writing projects.

How to Keep a Swipe File

A swipe file is a place where you store facts, figures, sentences and ideas relating to your work. It's a repository of information that if it's not relevant to your current writing project, will be of use at some point in the future.

Copywriters and advertisers use swipe files all the time to keep ideas, research and information that they can use for future campaigns.

Dan S. Kennedy is a legendary business author, copywriter and salesperson. He writes about swipe files, "I built up huge 'idea files'—samples of ads, mailings, and sales letters…You do not need much creativity to write letters; you only need to be adept at recycling and reorganising ideas, themes, words, and phrases."

I don't know about you but I'd rather become adept at this craft than be the type of person who grinds it out, project after project. If you're interested in learning more about copywriting, I explain how to write words that sell in a subsequent chapter.

If you keep a swipe file, the next time you have to write copy for a website, a blog post, an email or a social media campaign, you can take information directly from your swipe file instead of having to come up with fresh ideas. Swipe files means you can spend less time staring out of windows and more time accomplishing your non-fiction projects.

Don't think of swipe files as cheating either. Lawyers keep boilerplate legal text that they can use for future contracts and agreements. Professional software developers store snippets of code that can be used for future projects. Even journalists keep snippets from interviewees that they can use for future news stories.

As with a commonplace book, you can keep a paper or digital swipe file. A paper swipe file could consist of newspaper and magazine clippings as well as your notes that you store in a drawer next to your desk, or you could keep a digital swipe file using tools like Evernote.

Here are some of the more popular types of information productive writers keep in their swipe files:

- Headlines
- Quotes
- Interviews with people in your area of interest
- Inspiring videos and pictures
- Random facts and figures
- Sketches
- Phone numbers
- Angles for blog posts

- Emails
- Writing prompts
- Great first lines
- Advertisements
- Social media posts
- Presentations

To get the most use out of your swipe file, take time at the end of the week or before you're about to start a new writing project and see if there are any useful ideas that you can extract and turn into something fresh.

Why You Should Annotate What You Read

If you've ever picked up a dog-eared book from six or twelve months ago, you've probably had the experience of looking for half-remembered passages, quotations and arguments.

Annotating your favourite works means you can spend less time researching your current writing project and more time writing. It's a great way of critically engaging with whatever you're reading and ensuring this information seeps deeper into your subconscious.

I annotate books by highlighting passages on my Kindle. I also record observations about what I've read in digital apps like Evernote.

There's nothing wrong with making notes using pen and paper. You can do this in a journal, or you can underline favourite sentences in books.

These highlights, bookmarks and annotations can become food for future works. They enable you to connect the concepts in one book to another and examine how the author's writings relate to your life or your work.

Some experts recommend writing a brief summary after finishing a chapter so you can assess the value of a book later. I use this method when I want to remember something—for an exam, for example—but I rarely do this when I'm reading for relaxation.

When I'm writing an article or blog post, I return to my annotations for inspiration, for advice and sometimes to back up a point.

Prior to making annotations, I used to spend a lot of time searching old books for quotes that I half-remembered and points I wasn't sure about. Now, I can save time on research and spend more time writing.

Getting into the habit of annotating what you read and love is a great way of emulating and learning from the writing techniques of more accomplished writers. At the very least, annotations will help you consider what makes for a good sentence or argument and what makes for a poor one.

Write Your Ideas Down

Whether you use a commonplace book, a swipe file or just a notebook, get into the habit of writing your ideas down every day.

Lots of accomplished writers are fastidious about recording their ideas throughout the day.

Mark Twain carried a pocket notebook with him at all times for his ideas.

Thomas Jefferson jotted down notes about everything from the growth of plants and flowers to observations about daily life.

Even George Lucas keeps a notebook with him when he's shooting a film.

My favourite story about a writer who made it a point to write things down involves the children's author, Roald Dahl.

One day, Dahl found himself stuck in traffic. Suddenly, he thought of a breakthrough for a story he was working on. Having no notepad or pen, he grew afraid he'd forget his idea before getting home.

So, Dahl got out of the car and with his finger, he wrote the word 'chocolate' into the dirt on his vehicle. This act was enough for Dahl to remember his idea, and later it became *Charlie and the Chocolate Factory*.

He later said about his ideas, "You work it out and play around with it. You doodle… you make notes… it grows, it grows…"

Today, it's easier than ever to keep a portable notebook for recording ideas on the go. You can use digital tools, like an app on your smartphone, or you can buy a small notebook that fits in your pocket.

Whatever your tool, your notebook should become an extension of yourself.

6

HOLD YOURSELF TO ACCOUNT

"When the beginnings of self-destruction enter the heart it seems no bigger than a grain of sand." – John Cheever

HOLDING YOURSELF TO account means taking time to see how your writing is progressing and if you are working on (or writing) the right things. To follow this strategy, you must be realistic about your progress and growth as a writer and find a way to keep yourself honest.

There are two great methods productive writers can use to hold themselves to account.

The first is to **set clear goals** for your writing projects that you track and make progress towards each week. This method is suited for people who like lists and clearly defined boundaries.

The second method is to **keep a journal** where you write introspective entries about your writing. This method is best suited for writers who dislike the confines of a To Do list but still require a way to review how their work is progressing.

In this chapter, I'll explain how you can use either method to hold yourself to account.

Setting Goals

Setting goals in advance will give you something to work towards and help you eliminate non-essential tasks from your life. I like goals because they give a clear marker that I can work on making progress towards. In other words, I can either achieve a goal or miss it.

It's easy to set goals for your writing projects too. All you have to do is make sure they are SMART, that is:

(S)pecific: be clear about what exactly you want to achieve. 'I want to write a book' is not specific. 'I want to publish a collection of children's short stories' is.

(M)easurable: have a system for measuring your progress towards your goal each week or month.

(A)chievable: pick a goal that you can accomplish. If you haven't written much before, you're unlikely to write a novel in 3 months no matter how productive you are.

(R)ealistic: you must have a reasonable chance of accomplishing your goal. Winning the Nobel Prize for Literature is an unrealistic goal for most of us.

(T)imed: set a deadline for yourself that you can meet.

Here is one of my creative SMART goals:

I will self-publish (realistic) and sell (achievable) a short story collection (specific) by my birthday (timed, measurable).

Here's another SMART goal:

I will write 1,000 words a day or write 10 hours a week (measurable and specific) every week (achievable, realistic) before June 31st (timed).

Achieving Your Goals

Now comes the nuts and bolts of doing your work.

Here's what you need to know:

Each of your creative projects should have an outcome, that is a statement of how you want things to turn out.

Next, **write down all the actions** that you need to take on a list to achieve this outcome.

You can keep a separate list for each project or you can keep one master list with your tasks organised by context.

When writing your 'To Dos', use active verbs that are clear and specific so you don't have to think about them when you read them later on.

For example, when I'm planning my writing for the week, one of my action items will say, "Write a 1,000-word scene set in a restaurant on Thursday."

When I finish my blog post about productivity, my action item will say, "Email my latest blog post about productivity to my list by Wednesday."

Here's the kicker:

You don't need to do everything on these lists.

Instead, simply get everything down in one place, so you don't waste mental energy thinking about what you need to do during the week.

Then, once a day, once a week or as often as is necessary, pick the most important tasks from these lists and do them.

Here's what I do:

At the end of each day, I pick the three most important things I need to do the following day and focus on accomplishing these tasks first thing.

Finally, put the deadlines for each of these actions in your calendar so you can keep track of what's coming up. Use whatever works and stick with it and don't overthink it. It's often easier to obsess about how you're going to do the work than it is to do it.

The All-Seeing Gaze of Journal Writing

Don't like goals or To Do lists?

Don't worry, lots of writers find them confining. There's a simple writing practice you can use to gain an insight into how your writing is progressing. It's called journal writing.

Keeping a journal will foster your creativity and help you write more often. It's also a great way of holding yourself to account.

Why?

It's easy to talk about ourselves and our day, and writing a journal can help you turn thoughts and feelings into words and ideas.

Because a journal is private, you're less likely to censor yourself. This kind of honest writing is key to improving your craft and expanding the boundaries of your writing. And if you keep a journal for several years, older entries serve as signposts for how your writing is progressing.

You can keep a journal in a paper notebook, in a password-protected file on your computer or by using one of the many journal apps available for smartphones. In it, you could describe how your current writing project is progressing, what's holding you back and your plans for future. You could also use your journal to note sentences that you'd like to use and to tease out ideas for your writing projects.

The American novelist and short story writer John Cheever kept one of the best journals of the 20th century, and he wrote like one good friend talking to another. Throughout his life, he chronicled his difficult marriage, his loneliness, sexuality, alcoholism and decline.

Virginia Woolf was also fastidious about her journal writing as a means of holding herself to account. In an entry dated 1919, she described how journal writing encouraged and improved her craft.

"I believe that during the past year I can trace some increase of ease in my professional writing which I attribute to my casual hours after tea."

My life isn't much like Cheever's or Woolf's, but I learnt a lot about the art of journal writing from both authors.

Journal writing doesn't mean recording a daily summary of one's life. Anyone interested in writing a journal should expose themselves entirely in their journal and seek out brutal honestly.

I write about what I accomplished and failed at recently and what I'm thinking about. I also write about ideas for future writing projects. Some of my journal entries are only one or two lines long.

My shortest entry simply reads 'Exhausted'. (Did I mention that I have two small children?)

Others run several paragraphs or even pages in length.

The journals of Cheever and Nabokov taught me that keeping a journal helps identify negative patterns, thoughts and behaviours. In a way, journal writing is like the all-seeing gaze of Sauron in *Lord of the Rings*. You can't hide, and you can't run from it.

Woolf writes about her depression at length in her journals. In 1934, she describes the period after she finished her experimental novel The Waves.

"I was, I remember, nearer suicide, seriously, than since 1913."

John Cheever chronicles his alcoholism at length in his journal, and it's hard not to feel a sense of relief when he writes about finally becoming sober.

I don't want to be too morbid here.

The journals of these authors aren't all filled with dark life lessons and lamentations.

Nabokov writes at length about his love for his mother and father, his son and Russia of old. And I've yet to read a more powerful personal mission statement than Cheever's aspiration for the blank page:

"To write well, to write passionately, to be less inhibited, to be warmer, to be more self-critical, to recognise the power of as well as the force of lust, to write, to love."

Keeping a Sense Diary

Keeping a **sense diary or journal** is a useful practice for more creative writers who want to hold onto their experiences and ideas.

In it, record one sensual experience per day, like how a meal tasted or what a person's voice sounded like. Take notice of the stickiness of sweet tea, the coarseness of an unvarnished floor, and the pain behind your eyes when you're tired. The world is your source material.

Now, see if you can remix your sense diary to describe how a smell tasted or what a sound looks like. This may sound daft, but it's an unusually effective creative trick.

Synaesthesia is an accepted process for perceiving one sense in terms of another. It is also common practice for creative writers to remix and play on our perceptions of the five senses in their works.

Vladimir Nabokov, the Russian author of *Lolita,* described to the BBC in 1962 how he could hear colours in different languages.

He said, "The long 'a' of the English alphabet has for me the tint of weathered wood, but a French 'a' evokes polished ebony."

Go With What Works

I set goals for each of my writing projects and I keep a journal. I set goals because this keeps me honest and I find some comfort and security in having a To Do list that I can review, tick off and manage.

I also keep a journal. I like journal writing because it allows me to practice writing when I want to do anything but, and when I re-read older entries, I can unearth problems in my creative and even my personal life.

Use what works for you and abandon what doesn't.

7

STUCK? KEEP READING

"Either write something worth reading or do something worth writing." – Benjamin Franklin

ARE YOU STUCK in the Dark Ages?

If you don't read regularly, you are.

The German blacksmith Johannes Gutenberg invented the printing press sometime before 1450. His invention enabled the printing of lengthy texts that people were able to use to spread their ideas. In 1518, the theologian Martin Luther used Gutenberg's invention to print German copies of his Latin book 95 Theses. The subsequent popularity of this book across Europe became one of the driving forces of the Protestant Reformation.

Gutenburg's printing press enabled the dissemination of ideas that opened up people's minds to new ways of thinking and looking at the world, and it's a classic example of just how powerful ideas and books are.

If you want to become a better and more productive writer, you must read often and outside of your comfort zone.

Reading and writing have a symbiotic relationship. Through reading, you will discover stories, facts and arguments for your work and you will find new ideas and make connections that will improve your writing. The Bulgarian writer and critic Maria Popova describes this process as "combinatorial creativity."

She writes "…in order for us to truly create and contribute to the world, we have to be able to connect countless dots, to cross-pollinate ideas from a wealth of disciplines, to combine and recombine these pieces and build new castles."

Even if you read for pleasure, every time you open a book, you make an unconscious deposit in your memory bank of ideas.

However, if you don't read at all, the next time you turn up in front of the blank page your memory bank of ideas will be empty, and you will find it impossible to write anything meaningful.

How Benjamin Franklin Worked and Read

Benjamin Franklin is one of the modern age's most famous productive geniuses.

The United States Founding Father used the printing press to spread his ideas, and he even invented a more modern version of this device to grow his printing business. Alongside work, Franklin put aside several hours every morning and evening for reading and self-examination.

Each morning he asked himself: "What good shall I do today?" Franklin also advocated a daily 'air bath' instead of bathing in cold water.

He said about air baths, "I rise early almost every morning, and sit in my chamber without any clothes whatever, half an hour or an hour, according to the season, either reading or writing.

This practice is not in the least painful, but on the contrary, agreeable; and if I return to bed afterwards, before I dress myself, as sometimes happens, I make a supplement to my night's rest, of one or two hours of the most pleasing sleep that can be imagined."

Air baths won't help you write (or keep clean for that matter), but Franklin's life demonstrates how we can manage our downtime and incorporate important activities like reading and self-examination into our busy days.

For example, lots of people read at the end of the day. There's nothing wrong with this approach, but if you have a job and family commitments, at the end of the day you may lack the energy or patience for a challenging read. This, perhaps, is one reason why Benjamin Franklin made time for reading in the morning and afternoon.

Finding Time to Read

Lots of people say they'd like to read more, but they don't have the time or the energy. If you're having this problem, carve out small parts of the day when you have the energy or time to read, such as first thing in the morning. You can also take advantage of those random blocks of free time that life sometimes presents such as the unexpected twenty-minute wait in the doctor's office, a railway station or an airport.

If you get into the habit of carrying a book or e-reader, you can read during a lunch break, over breakfast, after dinner or while waiting for an appointment. Committing to reading at least 20 pages every day is another great way of setting yourself up for success. After all, if you can't find time to read 20 pages, then how can you find time to write? Similarly, if you drive to work, you can read more by listening to audiobooks during your commute.

I love reading but like many people, I browse the internet when I should be reading, or I end up reading the wrong book altogether.

Let me explain:

When I read about a book that sounds interesting, this leads to a "I'd love to read that book, but I have to read this book first" moment. Then, I invariably forget the name of the interesting book. Keeping a running list of books I want to read helped me overcome this problem.

If you do this, when you're stuck for something to read, you can consult your list before you buy. This method shortcuts wandering around a virtual or bricks and mortar bookshop and buying a book because the cover, reviews, or discounts are impressive.

The First 50 Pages

Oprah Winfrey famously advises that if you don't like a book you should stop reading it after 50 pages. Her thinking is there are so many good books available—and more than anyone can read in one lifetime—so there's no point wasting time on a book because you feel like you should. You can take Oprah's advice one step further by reading samples of books that Amazon and other stores make freely available before you buy the book.

Some heavy readers advise concentrating on one book at a time because this increases your chances of finishing one book and moving on to the next.

I disagree.

Reading several books at once means you can alternate books when one becomes tiresome or a slog. Then, you can return to the first book when you feel refreshed. For this method to work, it's worth reading books from several different genres or combining fiction and non-fiction.

Personally, I find non-fiction books are best suited for daytime reading while fiction books make for ideal night-time reading. I've also found reading three books at once feels about right; any more becomes overwhelming.

There's a Great Sentence Waiting for You

Sometimes, I read several books at once over the course of a week or two. On other occasions, I go several weeks without reading any long-form works. This drought isn't because I don't want to read; it's because the challenges of a day-to-day life get in the way.

I used to feel guilty about these breaks from the written word, but now I accept them because I know I will return to a bookstore with my list and a belief that there's a great sentence waiting to be read.

Reading, like any activity, has its peaks and troughs, and rather than beating yourself up about not reading, accept there will be times when you don't have a lot of free time. And if you hate the damn book, put it down and start something new, something better.

As a productive writer, it's your job to read books that fall inside and outside your comfort zone. You can do this by carving out reading time in your day, making the most of those random blocks of free time we all have, and by keeping track of what you want to read.

The morning question, What good shall I do this day?	5	Rise, wash, and address *Powerful Goodness;* contrive day's business and take the resolution of the day; prosecute the present study; and breakfast.
	6	
	7	
	8	
	9	Work.
	10	
	11	
	12	Read or overlook my accounts, and dine.
	1	
	2	
	3	Work.
	4	
	5	
	6	Put things in their places, supper, music, or diversion, or conversation; examination of the day.
	7	
	8	
	9	
Evening question, What good have I done today?	10	
	11	
	12	
	1	Sleep.
	2	
	3	
	4	

Benjamin Franklin's original daily routine via http://www.usgennet.org/

8

GET PERMISSION LATER

"Never ask permission, ask for forgiveness later."
– James Altucher

MANY PEOPLE SAY they to want write, but then they make excuses. They say things like:

- "I'm not good enough to write."
- "Nobody will read or publish my work."
- "I've nothing to write about."
- "I just don't have enough time to write."
- "I'll write when I've more life experience."
- "I'll write tomorrow."
- "I'd write but I've got this thing to do."
- "I wasn't any good at English in school."
- "Writing is too hard."

Instead of waiting for some anointed writing guru on high to give you permission to write, start today.

School teaches almost nothing about writing, beyond how to read and spell. You can learn everything there is to know about writing by reading voraciously. You don't need years of life experience either; the American disability activist and author, Helen Keller published *The Story of My Life* when she was 22.

If you pick up the pen and sit down in front of the blank page, you are good enough simply because you've moved past the point of procrastination. This act is no small feat.

Today, successful writers don't need as much talent or luck as writers like John Updike or Ernest Hemingway had. We can write a blog post, article or book and then self-publish it. If we write, we can take advantage of the digital tools that our predecessors didn't have and share our work almost instantly with an audience.

You can write for someone's website, start your blog or self-publish a book on Amazon.

Don't wait for someone to give you permission.

Writing consumes a lot of time, but you can make this back by eliminating passive activities in your day. Television, casual internet browsing, social media and staying up late into the night—I'm looking at you.

After you eliminate these passive activities and get into the habit of regularly writing, your mind will fill the vacuum with new and more fantastic ideas clamouring for space on the page in front of you.

If you've really got something to do that's more important than writing, ask yourself why you want to write in the first place and then decide what's more important. It's going to be hard work, but if it were easy, it wouldn't be worth doing.

As soon as you turn up in front of the blank page with a desire to say something, anything, you're already ahead.

Stop making excuses and pick up the pen. Later, if you find the whole process a waste of time, you can cross writing off your list and move on with your life.

Why You Should Learn to Write for Yourself First

Several years ago, I spent a year studying creative and non-fiction writing in a popular Dublin workshop.

The tutor was a burnt-out, disillusioned and exceptionally talented writer who demanded to know why we had joined his class.

One student said, "I'm here because I want to get rich."

He wasn't joking.

The tutor took this student aside and gave him his money back.

Writing isn't a shortcut to celebrity or riches.

If that's your goal, you will find rewards far quicker by concentrating on other professions. There's some truth in the stereotypical image of a penniless and starving writer. I'm not suggesting writers should starve, but you must be passionate about your work.

If you are passionate about your work, this passion will sustain you when others criticise and reject you. This passion will drive you when you're struggling to make money from your words. And if you are passionate enough, you will keep seeking ways to improve even when you're exhausted, frustrated and broken.

If, on the other hand, you're not passionate about your writing, then why should your readers care?

Write for yourself first, write something that you enjoy reading and write something that makes you regard a page of wet ink (or a screen of pixels), a page you filled, with pride.

Use the life of J.D. Salinger as an example.

After the success of *The Catcher in the Rye*, J.D. Salinger withdrew from public view. In 1953, two years after the publication of his famous book, Salinger left New York and moved to a remote, 90-acre place in Cornish, New Hampshire. There, he withdrew from public gaze. He continued to write, but this time for himself, and some of these stories were only published after his death in 2010.

Others remain unpublished.

Salinger loved what he did, and he didn't care if people read his works.

Why You Don't Need Anyone Else to Write

I once coached a non-fiction writer about how he could focus on his work and write 1,000 words a day. We talked about how he could use a productivity strategy to eliminate distractions and increase his daily word count. And we discussed why separating writing and research makes sense for anyone who wants to finish writing what they started.

I think the writer was happy with how our coaching call went because afterwards he emailed me to say thanks.

At the bottom of his email he wrote:

"The other helpful thing was the sense of legitimacy as a writer I got from talking with you."

I was happy to get positive feedback like this (I'm human after all!) and to know I was able to help him in some small way.

But, something didn't sit right with me.

The more I thought about our conversation, the more I realised I'd missed an important point.

This writer was already doing his most important work before he had ever talked to me.

He is well on his way.

If you wrote today, you are too.

Whatever type of writer you are, you don't need validation from me or anyone else to call yourself a writer or to feel like what you are doing is worthwhile.

If you have the guts to turn up every day, to sit down in the chair and do the hard work of putting one word after another onto the blank page even when you know what you're saying may not be any good, then you are a writer.

Don't ask for permission.

Don't wait for someone to tell you what you're doing is worthwhile.

And don't do it for the money (but always make sure you get paid).

I spent most of my early twenties looking for validation from accomplished writers and professional editors.

I paid for writing courses and I made a point of getting closer to editors who I knew were better than I.

Sometimes I got the validation I was after, but more often than not I didn't.

Either way, I still had to sit down in front of the blank page alone, get the words down and figure out a way to get better.

Every day, I try to do what writers like Natalie Goldberg recommend:

"Write what disturbs you, what you fear, what you have not been willing to speak about. Be willing to be split open."

I still feel like giving up some days.

I almost gave up last week.

I'm still trying to figure out this strange job of ours.

Writing is often a lonely craft and it sometimes helps to talk to other writers about a problem you're having on the blank page.

Yes, it's great to be recognised and for someone to say your work is good.

We all need feedback and support to overcome our problems from time to time. The importance of critical feedback is why productive writers have or hire editors!

I love getting comments and emails from readers who have opinions and even nice things to say about my work.

I keep them in a file in my computer and re-read them when I feel like quitting.

I'd like to tell you I don't feel like quitting very often, but I'd be lying.

These comments and emails keep me going when I want to stop. And I must keep on putting one word after another because this is what we do.

If you take one idea away from this book, it's this:

To become a productive writer, turn up for, write and go after what you want day after day.

Even if you win the lotto tomorrow, and your money worries disappear, even if you're the lone survivor of a nuclear holocaust, sit down and do your most important work.

Do it because there's an ache inside you that only writing can soothe.

Do it because you can't imagine doing anything else.

Do it because to write is to create and to create is to live.

Anything else isn't an option.

9

STEAL FROM THE GREATS

"Good artists copy, great artists steal." – Pablo Picasso

Are you a thief?

If you're a writer or in any way creative, you should be.

There are over seven billion people alive on this planet today, to say nothing of those who went before us. To think that your idea is original is to ignore the weight of history. The Bible has been done, *War and Peace* is over, and *Moby Dick* has been harpooned.

I'm not special. My ideas are far from original. I wrote *A Handbook for the Productive Writer* because I've read so much good, bad and unusual advice about productivity and writing over the years. I wanted to put it down on the blank page and remix it with my voice and experiences. I wanted to learn from my idols and create something that would help readers, that would help you.

So I stole.

I'm not the first person to confess this crime.

Take Apple's co-founder, Steve Jobs. He is widely acknowledged as one of the most creative innovators of the past fifty years but Steve stole like crazy, and he openly admitted it.

You can watch a video of Steve on YouTube explaining why creative people steal.

He said, "Picasso had a saying—'good artists copy, great artists steal'—and we have always been shameless about stealing great ideas."

Jobs is widely credited as the inventor of the portable music player or iPod, but he wasn't the first person to invent a portable music player; the boffins at Sony were. Jobs wasn't the first person to invent a tablet either; there were dozens of BlackBerry and IBM models before the iPad. Instead, Jobs took ideas already in existence and remixed them with his voice. He took old ideas and transformed them into better ones.

Don't waste time sitting around stroking your chin, gazing at the night sky and trying to come up with something original. Somebody, somewhere has already written or thought about what you're about to say or think. Your job as a productive writer, is to take an old idea, add your voice and transform it.

How to Emulate Your Idols

The productive writer learns faster by emulating his idols.

This process is different from stealing or copying your heroes. When you emulate, you make a conscious decision to take apart the work of your idols and reassemble it using your voice and ideas. It's an educational process that will help you discover how accomplished writers succeed and fail on the blank page, and it will help you finish what you're working on.

"At some point, you'll have to move from imitating your heroes to emulating them," Austin Kleon writes in Steal Like an Artist.

When a mechanic wants to figure out an engine, he or she sometimes spends hours taking it apart and putting it back together. This process helps the mechanic see how the engine works and even what's wrong with it.

If you want to learn from your favourite writer, pick something they wrote that you admire. Take it apart sentence by sentence and ask yourself:

- How does the writer make you feel throughout the piece?

- Where does the writer use the first, second or third person?

- Does the writer address you directly or indirectly? How does this make you feel?

- How much of their work is fact, fiction or embellishment?

- How does the writer manage to convey their opinion or argument?
- How do they begin and end each sentence, paragraph or chapter?
- Do you agree with what the author is saying or could you say it differently? If so, how?
- How does the writer introduce a topic and arrive at a conclusion?
- When does the writer repeat themselves and why?
- What type of journey does the writer bring you on?
- Why has the writer structured their work one way and not the other?

You can do this by writing out the stories of your idols line by line, by annotating their work or even by extracting key quotes and ideas and putting them into your swipe file or commonplace book for future use.

Disassembling and reassembling the work of your idols will help you figure out how they construct their sentences, paragraphs, chapters, and ideas. This creative process is time-consuming, but it will help you develop your voice for writing, and it will give you an insight into how your creative idols liked to work.

What I Stole

The American poet, novelist and short story writer Charles Bukowski is one of my creative idols. His brash style of poetry makes me feel like he's picking a fight with me, and I've always been fascinated by his honest portrayals of writing, creativity, the drudgery of work and his relationships with women.

I took his work apart line by line by writing down key lines from his poems and using them as fragments and ideas for entries in my journal. I even used one of his poems as inspiration for a short story.

The short story writer Raymond Carver is another creative idol of mine. I've spent hours reading and rereading his collection of short stories, *What We Talk About When We Talk About Love* and *Cathedral*. I tried to mimic his manner of writing sparse and clean sentences and studied how he portrays a character, a scene, and a major plot point. I used what Carver knew about the art of the short story to expose weaknesses in my work.

My efforts at reconstruction fell short on both counts, but I discovered I'm more comfortable writing in the first person and using everyday language. I found out more about the mechanics of a great story, and I discovered the nuggets of ideas for my fiction and non-fiction.

Stealing Responsibly

The next time a writer impresses you, read them closely, emulate what they do and steal their best ideas.

I'm not advocating a cut-and-paste job; instead take what they've done and remix it with your voice. If you only take from one writer, it's outright theft, but if you take from the many, it's creative.

Use the creative hard work of your idols to provide a foundation for what you're going to write. Prop your ideas on the foundations of their hard work. Cite your sources and wear your inspirations on your sleeve if you need to.

Don't be ashamed about what you're doing either.

Creativity exists somewhere between a stolen idea and your inner voice.

You can use that.

10

ASK A DIFFICULT QUESTION

"In all affairs it's a healthy thing now and then to hang a question mark on the things you have long taken for granted."
– Bertrand Russell

WHEN WAS THE last time you opened with a question?

Writing is a tool of discovery. The next time you're struggling begin a piece, ask your readers (or yourself) a difficult question.

- What would happen if…
- How can I achieve…
- Why is she against…
- When will we stop…
- Which is the best …

If you try to answer your uncertainty, you can learn more about your topic, and if you share what you've learnt, your readers will follow.

Many blogs are built on the back of tutorials and guides where the blogger asks how to do something and then answers these questions. On my blog, I try to answer the question: "How can you accomplish more on the blank page?"

Popular self-help authors question why people act a certain way before offering their solution. Relationship counsellor and best-selling author, John Gray, answers the question: "Why are men and women so different?" in *Men Are From Mars and Women Are From Venus*.

Business writers ask readers what they want to accomplish before providing an answer. The business author, David Allen, built a career by answering the question: "How can busy people get things done?"

Even fiction authors seek to answer a question: Dickens wrote, "It was the best of times, it was the worst of times", leaving the reader with the question: "How can it be both?"

You don't have to know everything; you just have to be willing to ask a question and then spend time searching for an answer. Framing your work this way will help you reach the end of whatever you're working on, and it will attract readers.

We're not alone in our ignorance.

Go Wide, Go Deep or Go Home

Who doesn't love Wikipedia?

It's one of the world's most popular and free learning resources.

Like many older internet users, I remember when we had to pay serious money for an incomplete encyclopaedia. Now, we can find this information on sites like Wikipedia, and it's free. I can learn about the history of Senegal, the top ten American presidents, and every episode of Seinfeld in one browsing session.

Does that make me an expert in Senegalese history, American politics or television comedy?

No.

Wikipedia and sites like it offer up a vast stream of information. The stream extends far beyond what we can see, but when we wade in, this stream of knowledge doesn't rise much higher than our knees.

You can't become an expert in your field by reading a Wikipedia article. It's almost impossible to immerse yourself in a topic with writing that runs wide rather than deep.

If you want to become an expert, you'll have to pick up a book. Books succeed in ways that websites can't, because they offer a deeper kind of immersion. They offer expert, focused knowledge that you can drown in.

If you're writing for the web, go wide. A blog post reader or a website visitor doesn't necessarily have the time or inclination to drown in your expert knowledge. They have a limited amount of time– most website visitors spend less than ninety seconds on a page–and you've got even less time to convince them to stay.

If someone decides to read your book, they're offering you hours of their life. They're prepared to sit at length and concentrate on your words. So, give them everything you have. Let them sift through your expert knowledge, and show them that you deserve their time.

The trick is to know when to go wide and when to go deep. If you mix the two up, you may as well go home.

Know Why You Do What You Do

Writing is an odd profession.

Much of it involves sitting in a room by yourself for extended periods of time and trying to create something from nothing.

Other people in your life who are not writers or creative professionals may not understand why you do what you do.

You should.

One of the best ways to do it is to ask the question 'Why?' three times before you start any new creative project.

Each time you answer this question, you'll go a little deeper and discover more about your motivations.

For example:

'I want to write a book about productivity.'

Why?

'I want to build my knowledge about this topic and share what I learn with readers and writers.'

Why?

'I enjoy teaching and writing about productivity concepts.'

This is a personal example and I share it with you so you can see how helpful it is to understand 'why' you do what you do.

Know why you do what you do, and you can overcome creative problems like writer's block.

Focus on the Essentials

Essentialism means getting more of the right things done.

According to Greg McKeown, author of *Essentialism: The Disciplined Pursuit of Less*, an essentialist removes the trivial and focuses on what adds value.

They make smart decisions about how to spend their time, energy, and resources because they understand this is the best way of contributing more to the people in their lives, to their families, and to society. That sounds a lot like what the productive writer does too.

I've discovered five important questions that are helping me make progress toward getting more of the right things done.

And I want to share them with you.

Q. Is this Activity Adding Value to My Life?

Since I was a child, I played and loved video games. When I was in my mid-twenties, I even reviewed them for a popular entertainment website. The website didn't pay me, but I didn't care. I enjoyed gaming, and I was able to keep the games after I wrote my reviews.

After a year or two of this, I felt a shift in how I approached games. Instead of looking forward to playing the next AAA title or blockbuster release, I began to dread the tedious missions, the walkthroughs, and inevitable write-ups.

One morning, after staying up late gaming the night before, I woke up and realised I was wasting my time and energy on something I didn't enjoy. I emailed my editor and told him I was done. Then, I sold my games and gave my console to my son.

I'm not making a case against gaming; instead, I share this story as an example of how we value our time differently as we grow older.

Q. How Am I Going to Fill My Glass?

Consider your entire day as a glass:

You can fill this glass with important activities, or big rocks, such as spending time with family or working on projects you're passionate about. Then, you can fill the glass with non-essential activities like answering email or watching television—these are like grains of sand, and they will settle around the big rocks in your day.

If you fill your glass with non-essential activities first, there will be no room left for the big rocks in your day.

Every night, before I go to bed, I ask myself what I want to fill my glass with.

My answer is almost always the same: to write.

Unless I act, these grains of sand will fill my day and leave no room for writing. However, if I make a conscious decision to write, these grains of sand settle around the big rocks in my day.

I'm not going to lie and say I fit writing into every day, but when I do I feel lighter. And if I write first thing—even if it's just a journal entry—I don't have the inevitable moment when I sit on the couch after an exhausting and demanding day and think, "Oh no, I still have to write."

If you're not a writer, you still have big rocks in your life. Examples include spending time with a loved one, meditating, exercising, work and more. Your grains of sand may be commitments you've made to others that aren't adding value to your life or passive activities like watching the news or reading social media feeds.

Decide on your big rocks before you got to bed, and you will wake up and fill your day with what matters.

Q. What Clutter Can I Eliminate?

Two years ago, I lost a dream job. I was unemployed for six months, and spent a lot of this free time figuring out what matters most to me and reading about essentialism.

It felt like something I could get into, and when you're unemployed, you need something to get into. The quickest way to get started is to eliminate material goods you don't use, need, love, or depend on.

I sold my laptop because I prefer writing using my desktop computer. I donated every book to charity that I promised myself I'd read but had no intention of doing so. I got rid of every item of clothing that I hadn't worn during the past twelve months. And, I deleted almost all of the unwatched films and TV shows on my hard drive and cancelled subscriptions to various online services.

Later on, when I found a job, I thought of buying a new laptop and replacing the clothes I'd given away. But I found I didn't miss any of these things.

Eliminating clutter gave me more space, more time, and more room for the big rocks in my life.

Q. How Do I Protect Myself?

To be an essentialist is to protect your physical, mental, and spiritual health. Each of these three areas represents one side of a triangle, and if one is under stress, the other two will suffer.

Here's how I protect myself:

To look after my mental health, I expose myself to new ideas through challenging books and record ten ideas every day based on these books. This practice keeps my brain active.

To look after my physical health, I run up to twenty miles a week. This practice helps me work through stressful problems, and it gives me more energy for other areas of my life.

To look after my spiritual health, I try to meditate for an hour a week, and I write regular journal entries about what I'm struggling with and things I feel grateful for.

I find this practice exceptionally difficult, but taking a step back from the trenches of the working week helps me quiet my monkey mind. It helps me sleep better at night. And then I can return to whatever I'm doing with a renewed vigour.

Q: How Often Do I Disconnect?

Several years ago, I went on vacation to a campsite in Italy. There was no immediately available internet access at the campsite, and I wasn't able to check my phone and my feeds or read the news whenever I wanted.

On the first day of this trip, I felt disconnected and behind. My hands kept reaching for the email app on my phone even though I knew I didn't have access to the internet.

After a day or two this habit died, and I began to enjoy these disconnected few days away from home. I took one lesson home from this holiday.

Being constantly connected kills my opportunity to escape, to enjoy a vacation, to spend time with the people I'm with and even to focus on my work.

It's been a while since I've gone a week without email, but I've removed the email app from my phone and only check it at predefined periods during the day. I've also disabled as many notifications as possible on the devices that I use. And I regularly work without being connected to the internet.

If you take regular time out to take care of yourself, you will be better able to focus on what matters.

Live Your Wild and Precious Life

An essentialist avoids spending their time on tasks they can say no to, on people they should say no to, and on compromises that aren't worth making.

They are committed to working on what inspires them, on what they're talented at, and pursuing their contributions to the world.

I'm still working on becoming an essentialist and eliminating the trivial from my life. It's a difficult practice and one I fall away from often, but I know the productive writer can live their wild and precious life if they're brave enough.

11

LEARN TO SAY NO

"It takes determination, it takes a willingness to say 'no' and it can take time. But it will pay off in so many ways, for the rest of your life." – Leo Babauta

WHAT'S THE BIGGEST barrier between you and a finished piece of work?

Look in the mirror.

There are not enough hours in the day and, if you're like most people, you probably have too many personal and professional commitments to balance writing with other larger ambitions. The vast majority of us have far more going on in our lives than we realise. All these commitments and projects carry a psychic weight.

This psychic weight slows your progress and makes it harder to reach the end of whatever you're working on.

For example:

Can you concentrate at length on your novel or book if you also have to manage a large DIY project?

If you attend a late dinner with friends and go for drinks afterwards, will you be able to rise early in the morning to write?

How productive will you be on the blank page if you've already worked overtime to pay for a new television?

Learning to say no to internal and external commitments is key to becoming a more productive writer.

If you decide to learn a new language, develop a new skill or take up a new hobby, you are taking time away from writing. These new hobbies and skills may add value to your life, and you may be able to juggle some of these commitments, but writing is a demanding mistress, and she needs your attention.

Can you afford to spend your valuable free time elsewhere?

Every new project you begin represents time you won't spend in front of the blank page. These new commitments can clog your creative bandwidth and reduce your ability to focus on the blank page.

By saying no, you can fence the parts of your day that you spend writing and concentrate on finishing what you started.

In *Daily Rituals: How Artists Work*, Mason Currey describes how the French novelist, Marcel Proust "made a conscious decision in 1910 to withdraw from society" and concentrate on his work.

Curry notes Pablo Picasso and his girlfriend, Fernande Olivier, regarded Sunday as an "at home" day, free from the obligations of friendship.

You don't need to be a recluse to become a more productive writer. Instead, consider how you're spending your time and if the result is worth the effort.

Apply Pareto's Principle

In 1906, the Italian economist Vilfredo Pareto found that 80 percent of the land in Italy was owned by 20 percent of the people.

Today, Pareto's Principle is the approach that anyone, including writers, can use to become more productive. It states that 20 percent of what we do provides 80 percent of the value we experience in our lives.

You can apply this method to your writing by considering what activities in your life are meaningful and what you can eliminate or reduce. Your goal should be to concentrate on those 20 percent activities that give you 80 percent of the value that you experience.

For example, it's more productive to spend an hour every day writing than it is to spend this hour promoting your work on social media.

Look for secondary activities that you can eliminate from your life.

Examples include: watching television, browsing social media sites, comfort eating, online shopping and so on.

This is a point the self-published authors, Johnny B. Truant and Sean Platt, address in their self-publishing guide *Write. Publish. Repeat.*

"Eighty-percent activities are writing more and better books, building a moderate amount of reader engagement (efficiently, not via long emails), creating solid calls to action that lead people to your next books from the backs of those they've just finished, completing bundles and product funnels…and so on," they write.

When I'm writing, I reduce the amount of time I spend watching television, gaming and browsing my favourite websites so I can spend more time writing.

I don't always succeed, but Pareto's Principle helps me refocus when I falter.

For example, when I began building an online platform for my writing, I became preoccupied with learning to code. I spent a lot of time teaching myself HTML, CSS, JavaScript and the backend of WordPress. I also took various online classes in Illustrator, Photoshop and other design applications. I wrote reviews about my experiences and even considered started a blog about coding.

What happened?

This type of learning served me well, and I learnt something of effective design. I also had less time to write the kind of prose that inspires me, and I produced fewer blog posts and articles.

I was putting more time and effort into design and coding activities and experiencing less meaningful results. I've never had ambitions to become a serious coder or a designer and these activities, while useful, are side attractions.

Now, I outsource any technical aspects to my blog on sites like oDesk.com. I also spend less time concerning myself with the design of my site. Instead, I rely on premium WordPress themes and plugins that take care of the hard work for me. This way I can spend more time writing and finish what I started.

Before you say yes to your next project, consider if the project is a 20 percent that will provide real value later on. Then make your decision.

Using No to Get More Done

If you want to become a more productive writer, make friends with the word No. It will help you avoid getting distracted, get out of unnecessary commitments and spend more time writing. Saying no to non-essential tasks will enable you to become a more productive writer.

Three Famous Writers on Why Creative People Say No

It's not rude, impolite or anti-social to say no. Creative people say no all the time: First there's Charles Dickens:

"'It is only half an hour'—'It is only an afternoon'—'It is only an evening,' people say to me over and over again; but they don't know that it is impossible to command oneself sometimes to any stipulated and set disposal of five minutes—or that the mere consciousness of an engagement will sometime worry a whole day."

Next, there's Saul Bellow. According to his secretary, he said:

"Mr Bellow informed me that he remains creative in the second half of life, at least in part, because he does not allow himself to be a part of other people's 'studies.'"

Saul once said about his decisions to often say no:

"I placed the highest priority on the sort of life that lets me focus on writing, not associating with all the people around me."

Say No to the Wrong Types of Writing Projects

For several years, I reviewed products and services I had no interest in because a newspaper paid me for it. This mindless writing stopped me creating the type of fiction and non-fiction that inspires me.

As a writer, you'll have lots of chances to exercise your creative muscles.

It may feel good to write an email, a page of copy or even an article (we all need to get paid), but what are your larger ambitions for the blank page?

Is this writing project going to get you there?

Say No to Good Ideas

The more often you write, the more connections your brain will make between pieces of information you pick up during the day.

Your brain will spit out ideas for articles to write about, projects to take on and opportunities to purse. Some ideas will be good, some terrible and others plain daft.

It's easy to refuse a terrible or a daft idea, but it's harder to refuse a good idea.

Here's the problem:

If you pursue every good idea, you won't have time or space for the great ideas.

The next time you've got a good idea, ask if it's worth pursuing and if it's something you should be really writing about.

Say No to New Writing Tools

Confession: I love new writing tools[1].

I've spent hours testing writing apps, online services and even the perfect desk and chair.

Like lots of writers, I find the tools of the craft exciting to discover.

Some tools help me become more productive, but when I start using a new tool for the first time, it interrupts the flow of writing.

These tools are side attractions that distract you from the main event.

Say No to Boring Books

Are you reading a boring book? Are you past page 50? Put it down and move onto something more exciting.

Get out of the genres that make you feel at home and away from your old reliable authors.

They have their purpose, but creative people go in search of fresh and challenging ideas. They find them in unexpected places.

Say No to Unproductive Habits

Do you stay up late at night watching television? Is Facebook taking up your time? Or perhaps you're spending your attention checking emails on your phone?

---

1   http://thebookdesigner.com/2015/04/bryan-collins/

These unproductive habits are draining your mental energy.

Consider only using social media at predetermined periods and removing email entirely from your phone (I did this and I haven't looked back) and making a commitment to your creative work over all else.

How To Say No Like a Pro

Now you have an idea of what to say no to, but how can you do it without offending your spouse, boss or friend?

Be firm but polite.

If you feel under pressure to say yes, explain to the person you're saying no to that you're working on an important writing project and you're close to a deadline. You'll return to their request as soon as you're free.

Then, make a point of doing so.

Give the appearance of having said yes.

When someone makes a request, like a manager asking for a report, don't attend to it immediately unless it's urgent.

Write this request down on your To Do list and get back to writing. Then, when you've finished, review your To Do list and evaluate which requests you need to act on.

This way you can say no to the interruption while giving the appearance of having said yes to the person.

Do your most important work first.

Let's say you get up early to write or work on a creative project.

Now if somebody makes a time-consuming request during the day, it doesn't matter if you can't refuse them. You'll already have completed your creative work.

You are ahead.

Get the Support of Your Boss

If you're a professional writer[2], part of your job is to tell your editor about your commitments.

Then, if your editor asks you to work on something you can politely decline and point to your commitments.

---

2   http://thebookdesigner.com/2015/04/bryan-collins/

Do less but better.

Set clear boundaries at home

If what you're writing is more personal, make it clear to friends and family members that you write at a certain time every morning or every night.

Stephen King describes this in On Writing, saying writers must "write with the door closed."

At first, family may come to you during these times to ask a question or make a request, but here's the kicker:

If you explain your passion and if they see your commitment, the people close to you will respect the time you're spending writing.

Guard Your Time like a Jealous Lover

As a productive writer, the word no is your most powerful weapon against the time-consuming demands of day-to-day life. You can use the word no to keep meaningless activities from filling your day and to prioritise what's important in your life. Saying no will help you become the productive writer you're meant to be.

12

WRITE WITHOUT FEAR OR FAVOUR

"I wrote and wrote without pause without consciousness of my surroundings hour after hour. I felt a different person...I didn't feel frustrated or shut up anymore. I was free, I could think, I could live, I could create..." – Christy Brown

SOME PEOPLE LOVE you.

Other people hate you.

Most people don't care.

There's so much information out there these days that your voice is just one of many shouting, "me too."

The growing glut of information is why there's no point holding back when you write.

If you tone down an article because you're afraid of what people will think, remember that most people are too wrapped up in their lives to care about one more blog post, article or book.

Yes, some of your friends and family might take issue with what you've got to say, but you're (hopefully) not writing to impress them.

You could take the easy road and try to convince people that you're a good or honest person (maybe you are), but if this results in a bland, generic piece of work, then you've wasted your time.

If you convince a reader to spend time with you, respect that they're giving finite hours of their life to you.

Whatever you have to say, it better be damned good.

The next time you sit in front of the blank page or screen, forget your reader's reactions. Write without fear of what your reader will think of you. If you find this difficult, you could:

- Write about your fears and use this as an entry point into your work
- Accept fear as a form of perfectionism that must be confronted
- Acknowledge your fears, accept them and write what you want
- Write a letter to a friend explaining what you're afraid about and then burn it
- Remember what the goal of your writing project is. Then move towards this goal one action or sentence at a time
- Write honestly now, edit for your audience later

When you publish your work, if you come across as compassionate and caring, so be it. If you come across as angry and insensitive, so be it. Your job as a writer is to call out to your readers and convince them to spend time with you.

If your writing is honest, it will be far more engaging than a piece where a writer holds back on revealing some essential truth because they're worried what others will think.

Don't Hide

If you use writing to hide yourself, then why should I spend time with you?

You know the type of writing I'm talking about.

You can find it on the promotional materials that came with your last bank statement or utility bill. You can read it on government documents and healthcare informational leaflets. It's there on thousands of corporate and institutional websites.

It's a joyless, staid type of writing that's full of passive verbs and awkward nouns. It comes from a world where nobody does anything to anyone and where no one cares. It talks about institutions and decisions. It tells me things firstly, and secondly, in hindsight, in conclusion, and after further deliberation.

All of it belongs in the bin.

I want to hear about the writer's problems and how they overcame them. I want to taste blood and feel the grit between my fingers. I want to take the author's outstretched hand and go on a journey.

I'm going to give you my time; please don't waste it.

The best kind of writers reveal some essential truth about the human condition; the rest of us aspiring writers can at least reveal some truth about ourselves.

I'm not asking you to slip into the confessional mode for every piece of writing; just don't make excuses for producing senseless copy that's devoid of life.

Even if you're writing copy for your business, don't bore me with paragraphs about your product's technical features. Don't expect me to sit through a thousand words of passive verbs, adjectives and nouns nobody ever says.

I've too many emails to answer, too many family commitments to keep, and there are too few hours in the day.

How are you going to solve my problems? Can you save me money or help me spend more time with my family? Show me how I can become rich or successful like you. Tell me something dangerous.

Then, I'll give you my time.

Christy Brown Did It, What's Your Excuse?

Christy Brown is one of Ireland's most famous writers and artists.

He grew up in inner-city Dublin during the middle part of the twentieth century, and he had cerebral palsy.

Christy was depressed for much of his life because of his disability and subsequent alcoholism.

He grew up in a large family, where he struggled to get attention because of his disability. So, with his mother's help, he learnt to write with his left foot. Later, as a young man, Christy wrote the famous memoir *My Left Foot*. He also published his ground-breaking novel *Down All the Days*.

I spent a year studying Christy Brown's life and works. What struck me most wasn't the power of his words or the way he overcame his disability; it was his ability to immerse himself completely in his craft and reveal an essential truth about life.

In *My Left Foot* Christy abandoned himself entirely to portraying what it was like to grow up with cerebral palsy and how his real disability lay in the reactions of those around him. In *Down All the Days,* Brown abandoned himself entirely to portraying how cruel, illogical and hard life was in Dublin during the mid-twentieth century.

Today, the significance of *My Left Foot* and *Down All the Days* may be understated, but their power and honesty remains intact. They are essential reading for anyone concerned with disability or with Irish literature. Brown offers more than just a glimpse of how he lived with disability; he expands our view of the world, and he reveals a fundamental part of the human condition. When Christy picked up his pen with his left foot, he abandoned himself entirely to the written word.

Both works contain a big idea and even if you the reader aren't prepared to climb on board, Brown commits himself entirely.

Although Christy never quite overcame his depression, he found a new, inner life through his creations and expressions on the blank page. This means today Brown's readers can share in this life long after his death.

Any aspiring writer can think and live and create on the blank page. We can stop making excuses and abandon ourselves to an idea. We can all learn from Christy Brown.

What New Writers Need To Know About Fear

When I was in my early twenties, I told people I wanted to write a book. There was just one problem. I wasn't writing anything, at all.

I believed I wasn't ready to write and that I needed some anointed mentor to pull me aside and say, "Bryan, now is your time."

I became jealous of the success of people around me and grew sick of my lack of progress.

So, I joined a fiction and non-fiction writing workshop in Dublin. On the second evening, the instructor said every student had to submit a short story.

I was afraid.

I hadn't written a short story in years, but I didn't want the class or the instructor to know this.

A writer in a writing class who doesn't write is a fraud.

I went home, and I wrote. I wrote that night and the night after that. And I wrote until I finished my first story. It was terrible—the instructor told me this later on—but it didn't matter.

I had taken the first step towards facing my fears.

Fear: I Don't Know Where to Start

Starting is tough.

For years, I couldn't start. I'd open up my word processor and then switch to my internet browser for research. I'd answer my email, or see if there was something I wanted to buy on Amazon. Afterwards, I'd check my bank balance and feel depressed.

It went on like this until I disappeared down a rabbit hole of meaningless internet searches and doing anything but the most important work of every writer.

Then, I learnt how to start by creating triggers for writing. These include making coffee, disconnecting from the internet and setting a timer to track how long I spend writing.

My routine for becoming a productive writer involves doing this at the same time each evening or morning. As a reward, I browse the internet, watch a movie or exercise. It's ritual, and it means I don't have to think about the act of starting.

To the outsider, this ritual looks boring, but it helps me write. That's more exciting than anything else I could do with my free time.

How to Overcome this Fear:

If you're having trouble starting, remember: it's your job to turn up and do the work. Once you've learned how to turn up, consider it a victory to write for 10 minutes without getting distracted. The next day, aim for 15 minutes. The day after, write for 20 minutes. Let these small personal victories accumulate over time and you will become a more productive writer.

Fear: Who Am I to Write?

While writing this book I was afraid others would say: "What right do you have to explain how to be productive?"

I still think that.

I also knew I'd spent hours researching productivity methods and studying how artists work. I'd read dozens of books by authors explaining how they work. And I knew enough to organise my thoughts into a book. Even though I am nobody, I gave myself permission to write a book because writers must start somewhere.

How to Overcome this Fear:

Give yourself permission to write. If this is difficult, remind yourself that everyone who wants to become a writer must start somewhere and that now is your time. Helen Keller wrote the Story of Her Life at aged 22. Anne Frank wrote her autobiography when she was just 15. Franz Kafka finished his first novel in his twenties. These are extreme examples.

I'm an extreme kind of person.

Are you?

Fear: I Can't Finish

Finishing is harder than starting.

When I was in my mid-twenties, I spent years struggling to finish anything. I wrote dozens of short stories and abandoned them. I thought of articles I wanted to write for newspapers, I researched them and then I never bothered to write them.

There wasn't any one moment where I learnt how to finish my work and become a writer. Instead, I got a job as a journalist writing for a newspaper. There, I had to finish my articles by a deadline because if I didn't the editor would fire me.

I know this because he called me into his office after I missed a deadline and told me.

I stopped polishing my articles until they were perfect and started finishing them. On more than one occasion, my editor sent the articles back to me saying I'd left out an important paragraph or that my introduction needed reworking.

This criticism made me want to quit.

On other occasions, the sub-editors of the paper reworked my article entirely. Having my work taken apart like this was brutal, but at least I was getting paid to write.

I learnt from their feedback, and I learnt by finishing what I started.

How to Overcome this Fear:

If you're having trouble finishing your work, set artificial deadlines and stick to them.

Enter contests and submit your articles to magazines or websites when these deadlines elapse. Make a public commitment to a group of people that you trust e.g. a writing group.

Start a blog.

As you get into the habit of finishing your work, you will win more opportunities to gain feedback about your work.

Fear: They'll Judge Me

I don't like personal writing like this. It's hard work, and it reveals more of me than a guide to the various writing tools I use. I almost deleted this chapter several times before I hit publish.

What's to enjoy about revealing a job didn't work out, that I was lazy, and that my work failed?

Stephen King made me do it.

In On Writing, Stephen King says:

"Write with the door closed, rewrite with the door open."

I could lock myself in a room and write about a caretaker of a hotel who goes insane and tries to kill his family. I could explain how to overcome the inertia of perfectionism. Or I could write about rejection.

How to Overcome this Fear:

Spend more time creating than you do consuming. Show the world what you created. And then let them judge it in all its ugly imperfections. Respond if you need to or move on. It's better to be judged than to be ignored.

People Are Going To Reject You (And Why This Doesn't Matter)

I was rejected three times while writing this chapter. I contacted five authors I admire with interview requests. Four of them said no. I asked several podcasting experts to share their advice for a guest blog post.

Half of them didn't reply. I pitched guest posts at the editors of three big blogs, two of whom said no.

These rejections are tough, but they are normal experiences for the productive writer.

If you want to become a productive writer, rejection waits for you at the beginning, in the middle and at the end of your work. It goes where you go. Everybody who succeeds gets rejected at some point during their careers.

By turning up and creating, you cut through your fears. Even if some people reject your work, others will embrace it. The next website you pitch may accept your ideas. You could win the next contest. Your next interview request may be granted.

You must write today. You must write now. You must write like your life depends on it.

Because it does.

13

SELL WITH WORDS

"Absolute truth is a very rare and dangerous commodity."
– Hunter S. Thompson

COPYWRITING IS WRITING that sells.

If the reader is not sold by the time they reach the last paragraph—or if they don't even read that far—the writing has failed and the writer goes hungry.

Great copywriting captures the reader's attention and persuades them to take action, and a great blog post should do the same.

As a writer, you may not always be persuading your reader to buy a product or service, but you sure as hell are persuading them to do something. You want them to give you their attention, believe that your ideas hold value, and take action on your advice.

Copywriting excels at this kind of persuasion. And while great copywriting is part art, the highly persuasive writing you've read on countless billboards, magazine advertisements, and online marketing campaigns is driven by tried and tested formulas that have worked for decades.

In this chapter, I'll give you two of my favourite copywriting formulas alongside some practical tips for selling with words.

How to Use PAS Formula To Sell

The simplest and most effective copywriting solution is the Problem-Agitate-Solution Formula or PAS. Copywriters have used this for years to put food on the table because it works. Let's break down this three-part formula:

- **Problem**: introduce a problem the reader is experiencing.
- **Agitate:** use emotional language to intensify the problem.
- **Solution**: offer a credible solution to the problem.

New writers who start a blog often complain about a lack of website traffic. As a result they feel frustrated and anxious about how they're spending their blogging time. Let's tackle this problem for these new writers:

[**Problem**] Are you sick and tired of writing articles and blog posts that nobody reads?

Now let's whip up our reader's emotions:

[**Agitate**] Millions of aspiring writers just like you publish posts every day, worry about SEO, and wonder if they should spend hundreds of dollars advertising on Facebook.

But unless you spend your time in the right places, you're never going to build the kind of audience you need to grow a successful blog.

Now we offer the reader a lifeline:

[**Solution**] What if I told you there's a better way? What if I told you guest blogging could help you attract thousands of new readers?

See how this formula uses a problem to draw the reader in?

How to Use the Approach Formula to Sell

Copywriters adapted this formula from a template often used by door-to-door salesmen. It's a soft sell where the writer works hard to make the right initial impression on the reader. The good news is it's easy to learn. There are six parts to this formula.

- Arrive
- Propose
- Persuade

- Reassure
- Make an offer
- Ask for the order

To use it, say something the reader will agree with—something non-threatening that shows you're both on the same page. Then, propose a certain course of action. Something that most people who agree with the arriving statement would find reasonable.

Next, gently persuade the reader that this course of action is the correct one. Finally, reassure the reader by overcoming any possible objections. Below, I've used this formula to convince new writers that it doesn't take long to master their chosen craft if they know where to start.

[Arrive] Becoming a great writer doesn't happen overnight.

[Propose] You know there's no quick fix or great secret to writing mastery—it simply takes practice. In fact, in his popular book Outliers, Malcolm Gladwell suggests that it takes 10,000 hours of practice to truly master a craft. But unguided practice is a terribly inefficient way to learn. That's why it may be time for you to hire a coach.

[Persuade] A writing coach will allow you to combine practice with the experienced feedback required to hone your skills in the fastest possible time. A writing coach will guide you past obstacles that will block you for hours, days, or even weeks working alone.

[Reassure] But if engaging a writing coach sounds complicated and expensive, don't worry—I'm going to keep this simple. In this post, I'll share the five things new writers should look for in a coach. I'll even show you how to get coaching for free.

I'm going to keep this simple: new writers who are ready to get help should look for five things from their next writing coach.

'But I'm Selling a Boring Product or Service'

Whatever you're selling with words, it's crucial to be able to tell a compelling story about your product or service and how it's going to improve the lives of your customers. Even if you're writing copy for a boring product or service, there's no reason you can't bring a sense of passion or excitement to your words.

The famous copywriter David Ogilvy wrote about the Rolls-Royce, "At 60 miles an hour the loudest noise in this new Rolls-Royce comes from the electric clock."

What's compelling about this example is Ogilvy's use of small details to bring this copy to life. He puts the reader right there in the car.

Here's another example:

Taking piano classes isn't the most glamorous way to pass time, but in 1926, John Caples wrote one of the most famous advertorials of all time about piano classes for the U.S. School of Music.

The headline for his famous advertorial reads, "They Laughed When I Sat Down At the Piano But When I Started to Play!"

Caples goes on to describe how, thanks to a course by the U.S. School of Music, he surprised his friends and family by playing the piano.

"I played on and as I played I forgot the people around me. I forgot the hour, the place, the breathless listeners. The little world I lived in seemed to fade—seemed to grow dim—unreal. Only the music was real."

This advertorial blurs the line between art and copy. This ad isn't just about learning to play the piano; it's about the power of music and how we all aspire to become better people. Caples' ad also demonstrates how a copywriter can use an emotional benefit of a product or service, tell a story and win over customers and readers.

Whether you're writing about consumer electronics, sports cars or a more boring product like an insurance product, the basics remain the same.

Grab 'Em By the Eyeballs

Your readers and customers won't click on boring, bland or unsexy headlines.

As a writer, it's your job to grab them by the eyeballs with an engaging headline.

If you're struggling to find a good headline for your article, take a look at magazine covers like *Cosmo*.

The writers for magazines like *Cosmo* are well-paid pros, and you can easily rework any of these proven headlines to suit your copywriting.

For example, I recently found the *Cosmo* headline *10 Sex Myths Busted!* and turned it into *10 Writing Myths Busted!* and I used the latter for a blog post.

Write at least ten headlines for every article you write and you will get better at the art of headline writing.

Use Everyday Language

Author and salesperson Dan Kennedy best explains why copy that sells must be simple and easy to read.

"I think sales letters should be reader-friendly. That means the letter appears easy to read, is easy on the eye, uses everyday language, and doesn't require you to be a Harvard grad or a determined masochist to get through it," he writes in *The Ultimate Sales Letter*.

I think of this sentence every time I pick up an indecipherable pamphlet from the insurance company, a jargon letter from the bank or a detailed brochure from my electricity provider. Most of the time these documents are impossible to read, and they almost always end up in the bin.

The next time you write copy for your audience consider: do you use everyday language?

Activate Your Verbs

One of the best ways to give your copy about a product or service more life is to shun the passive voice in favour of the active voice. In the passive voice, the subject (you) is acted on by a verb. It sounds weak, and you can usually spot the passive voice if a verb ends with -ed.

For example:

- It was decided
- The product was revealed
- A product is going to be
- In the active voice, the subject (you) performs the action. For example:
- We're releasing…
- We're announcing..
- We've just updated…

I'll cover the active voice in more detail in a subsequent chapter. However, if you're writing copy, it's enough to know that the active voice will make whatever you're saying sparkle and capture your readers' (or customers') attention.

Include a Call-to-Action

When you finish your copy, always call on your readers to act.

You could say:

- If you enjoyed this post, please share it on Facebook/Twitter/LinkedIn.

- Share your tips for [insert topic] in the comments sections below.

- Watch this free video/download this free resource to learn more about [insert topic here]

- Join the Insider list and get exclusive tips for [insert benefit here]

- Take out your 30-day free trial of [insert product] here

Go Out There and Sell Like a Pro

Copywriting is a skill like any other, and you've got to practice to improve. You can use the PAS, the Approach or another proven formula to sell products, ideas and services to your readers. I recommend saving great examples of copy into your personal file so you can see what works.

If you make a habit of writing copy and of studying how the experts sell with words, you'll naturally discover what sells and what doesn't work. You'll become the type of productive writer who knows how to build lasting relationships with readers and customers.

Supercharge Your Copywriting with These Power Words

Below are fifty top power words used by marketers and copywriters. These words work because they invoke emotion in the reader. There are hundreds more words like these.

If you write online, use Twitter to research the power words that work best for your ideas. You can do this by tweeting different headlines to the same piece of writing several hours apart and seeing which headlines perform best.

If you don't have a large Twitter following, study the most popular social media posts and blogs in your industry and take note of the emotional words the writers use in their headlines.

I also recommend visiting BuzzFeed. The headline writers of this popular entertainment and news website are masters of using power words and emotional language to encourage more people to click on their headlines.

Whatever your approach, a swipe file is an ideal place to store power words that work for you.

- Agony
- Astonishing
- Announcing
- Alert
- Beware
- Confidential
- Compare
- Devoted
- Download
- Evil
- Excited
- Extra
- Fearless
- Fortune
- Free
- Fulfil
- Genuine
- Gift
- Growth
- Guaranteed
- Happy
- Hero
- Insider
- Introducing
- Immediate
- Improved
- Important
- Jail
- Mind-blowing
- New
- Obsession
- Practical
- Private
- Prize
- Refundable
- Sale
- Security
- Sex
- Silly
- Strange
- Slaughter
- Sleazy
- Strong
- Tax
- Urgent
- Ultimate
- Unusual
- Valuable
- Zero

14

KNOW WHAT YOU'RE WRITING ABOUT

"We may be very busy, we may be very efficient, but we will also be truly effective only when we begin with the end in mind." – Stephen R. Covey

GREAT WRITING DOES at least one of four things. It entertains, educates, informs or inspires readers.

A news story is informative because it tell the reader something important about a current event. A tutorial is educational because it explains to readers how to accomplish a task. A short story is entertaining because it gives the reader a place where they can escape from their troubles. A self-help book is inspirational because it shows readers how they can change their lives for the better.

Before you start writing, decide if you want to entertain, inform, educate or inspire your reader. You don't have to achieve all four, but your writing should tick at least one of these boxes. If you don't, your reader will lose interest and put your writing down.

The good news is it's not as difficult as it sounds to give your readers what they want and hold their attention.

How to Inform Your Readers

Informing your readers means peppering your writing with research and facts that build credibility.

If you're writing for a publication, your editor will provide you with clear directions about what your writing should achieve and how you can give your readers what they want.

When I worked as a freelance journalist, I often received detailed briefs from editors explaining the topic I should cover, who I should interview and how long the piece should be.

Even if you're not working for an editor, consider yourself as a journalist who must examine a single topic with an unblinking gaze. As a journalist, you must be clear and level headed in your writing.

You must put some distance between your point of view and the facts. Informative writing means you'll be spending time interviewing experts and finding out unusual facts and information of interest to your readers.

How to Educate Your Readers

Educating your reader means adopting a personal and helpful tone. It's your job to put your hand around your reader's shoulder and say, "This isn't so hard to achieve, I can help you."

Examples of educational writing include tutorials, step-by-step articles, how-to guides, and even this book chapter.

You don't have to be an expert to educate your readers either.

Consider the curious case of the teenage maths student struggling with a difficult equation. Instead of asking the teacher for advice, he turns to his friend and asks him how to solve the equation.

In this case, the teenage maths student feels more comfortable asking his friend for advice because he can relate to his friend. This is because the two of them are at similar points along their learning journeys. You can use this principle to relate to your readers even if you're not an expert.

For example, in 2014 I ran the Dublin City marathon. It was my first marathon, and I'm not an expert at running or athletics and I would never profess to be. However, I could draw on the mistakes I made while training for this marathon to write an article like: 'Marathon Training Mistakes: 10 Lessons for Beginners'.

My beginner's article wouldn't interest serious runners, but a beginner considering their first race may be more interested in what I learnt because we're not so different.

If you are going to write an educational article that you want people to relate to, use clear and simple instructions the reader can follow. If you've ever read the instruction manual for an old appliance, you will appreciate how frustrating ambiguous instructions are. You should also provide practical tips free of jargon or opinion. This way, the reader can learn from your knowledge and decide for themselves what to do next.

Using metaphors the reader relates to will improve your writing too. A metaphor is a clever way of relating a concept to an everyday object or action. For example, "Running a blog is a lot like servicing a car because…" or "Writing a book is a lot like laying bricks because…" You can find another example of a metaphor in the chapter where I compare writing to making wine.

Finally, encourage the reader to persevere even when they feel like giving up. Remind the reader you were a beginner once too, and then show them what success looks like.

How to Inspire Your Readers

Inspiring readers is a different type of writing altogether. Often, this means drawing on personal stories and passions in your writing. It means invoking an emotion or change in your reader. It means persuading them to take action and even pushing them over the edge if they don't.

To inspire your readers, consider what your readers should feel after they read your work or what they should take away from your writing. Play on their fears and hopes. Paint a version of hell that they should avoid or describe a vision of the future as you see it. Give your readers specific examples of how you can both move towards your version of heaven together.

The most famous example of inspirational writing is Martin Luther King's I have a Dream speech, within which he paints his dream "that my four little children will one day live in a nation where they will not be judged by the colour of their skin but by the content of their character."

How to Entertain Your Readers

Entertaining the reader means drawing on personal stories that only you can tell. Yes, you can use humour, anecdotes, and clever wordplay, but story is king. It's the way we make sense of the world, and it's what people turn to when they want to escape from their problems.

The best way to entertain your readers is to tell a captivating story. There are entire books about effective storytelling, and I recommend reading *Story* by Robert McKee.

If you want to learn about story faster, one of the simplest and the best storytelling concepts is this six sentence fill-in-the-blanks template created by Pixar Studios.

Once upon a time there was... Every day... One day... Because of that... Because of that ...Until finally ...

Here's how this storytelling template works for the popular animated Pixar film *Finding Nemo*:

Once upon a time there was ... a widowed fish, named Marlin, who was extremely protective of his only son, Nemo. Every day ... Marlin warned Nemo of the ocean's dangers and implored him not to swim far away. One day... in an act of defiance, Nemo ignores his father's warnings and swims into the open water.

Because of that ... he is captured by a diver and ends up in the fish tank of a dentist in Sydney. Because of that ... Marlin sets off on a journey to recover Nemo, enlisting the help of other sea creatures along the way. Until finally ... Marlin and Nemo find each other, reunite and learn that love depends on trust.

How about this?

Once upon a time there was a new writer who couldn't finish what he started. Every day, he tried to write but kept getting distracted. One day, his editor boss fired him because he wasn't able to ship his work on time. Because of that the writer almost went broke. Because of that, he taught himself how to find better paying freelance contracts and get more things done. Until finally he made a habit of finishing what he started and got paid for his hard work.

Beginning With Your Readers in Mind

The writer who starts a project without knowing what they want to accomplish will find their work hard, slow and awkward.

Deciding the purpose of your work or beginning with the end in mind, before you put words onto the blank page, will give confines within which to write. It will give you a goal to write towards and help you finish what you started.

Remember, most readers are hungry for information and for a perspective that only YOU have.

If you want to become a more productive writer, give it to them.

15

STOP SEARCHING FOR THE PERFECT WRITING TOOL

"Do not wait; the time will never be 'just right'. Start where you stand, and work with whatever tools you may have at your command, and better tools will be found as you go along."
– George Herbert

THE PRODUCTIVE WRITER knows the perfect writing tool doesn't exist.

Ernest Hemingway wrote drafts of his works standing up with a pencil and paper.

Lewis Carroll declined a chair in favour of standing while writing.

Vladimir Nabokov, the Russian-American author of *Lolita,* wrote drafts of his novels on index cards and gave them to his wife to organise.

Every accomplished writer has their routine and idiosyncrasies. Writing while standing up may have worked for Hemingway and writing on index cards may have worked for Nabokov, but that doesn't mean these writing practices will work for you.

By all means, study how the greats completed their works but don't let your search for the perfect writing tool (or the perfect approach to writing) get in the way of producing more words.

For years, I was obsessed with finding the perfect writing tool. I told myself things like:

"When I get this piece of software, I'll be able to write more."

"This computer is the one I'm going to finally write a book with."

"I need the perfect writing space."

Computers make for more productive writing, but there is no perfect writing tool. Just as a bad tradesman blames their tools when they botch a job, a bad writer blames his or her tools when they can't accomplish something on the page.

Some writers even find computers confining. Steven Pressfield, author of *The War of Art*, prefers writing on his Smith-Corona typewriter over a computer, for example. I'm a digital writer at heart, but Pressfield's work habits are understandable. The blink of the cursor and the lure of distractions like email, social media and the internet place boundaries around a writer's creativity and productivity.

If you're having problems working a piece out, try writing for 30 minutes with pen and paper before returning to your computer. I've found this method forces me to write slower and stay with a thought for longer.

Find and use what works, and accept it in all its imperfections.

The Internet Is Not Your Friend

If you're a writer, the internet is not your friend, and this is coming from someone (me) who spends most of my time writing for the web! I'm not alone in this assertion.

During a book tour for his 2012 novel Freedom, the American novelist Jonathan Franzen, told a journalist he wanted to write more each day, so he physically removed his Wi-Fi card from his computer and permanently blocked his machine's ethernet connection with Super Glue.

I'm not suggesting that you wreck your machine or that an internet-free life is the path to becoming the next big thing. But disabling your internet access, even for short periods, will help you accomplish more on the page. Think of your internet-free writing sessions as a respite from the deluge of information we're presented with every day.

If you need to use the internet as part of your writing, make a point of conducting this kind of online research after you've completed your writing for the day.

I've never written anything of consequence while navigating from one site to the next. There are just too many distractions, too many feeds, too many unchecked emails, too many pings and too many responses. The blank page doesn't stand a chance in the face of a digital crowd clamouring for our attention.

Writing offline can feel liberating and intimate. There's no subconscious tug at the back of your mind to log into an account or refresh a feed. There are only your words and ideas.

Done? Great, Now Tidy Up

A master craftsman tidies up after themselves and prepares their work for the following day in advance. They do this because they know creativity is a long-term game, and it's their job to turn up day after day and do the work.

Ernest Hemingway, for example, stopped writing in the middle of a sentence so he'd know where to resume the following day.

You don't necessarily need to stop writing in the middle of a sentence, but it's helpful to have a clear idea of where you want to resume tomorrow. Perhaps you want to finish your introduction, expand on a certain chapter in your book or work on an outline?

Tidy up your work, organise your notes, and put your tools away. Tip the waitress in the coffee shop if you need to.

Make it easier to find the clear space you need to write again tomorrow, to improve your craft day after day.

Recommended Tools for the Productive Writer

There are hundreds of writing tools available today, and I can't possibly include every tool in this book. Instead I've picked the most popular and useful writing tools that I've used recently.

You've probably used some of these tools before, but if you haven't, they can help you write and finish whatever you're working on.

Word isn't sexy, but the Office suite is Microsoft's cash cow, and Word is the most popular writing application in the world today. If it wasn't for Word, we wouldn't have one of the most commonly used proprietary formats of all time: .DOC (that's not necessarily a good thing).

If you've written or read anything of note on a computer, you've used Word. Even if you're not reading a document on a screen, it was probably typed up or printed in Word at some point. Word has been around in one form or another since 1981. It's had a hell of a head start.

Like many people, I have a love/hate relationship with this programme. It's overpriced, and it's prone to crashing on certain machines. Laying out a document with pictures and tables is a fresh kind of hell. Word is difficult to master in that it does so many things in so many different ways. That said, Word can do far more than any writer would ever want. It's the default word processor in many modern offices for a reason.

Scrivener was built with writers in mind. It is available on Windows and OS X, and I used it to plan and write this book. This application excels if you are working on a long or complicated document like a thesis, book, novel, paper or college essay.

Scrivener lets you to manage, edit and write multiple documents at once. It also provides a place to store research notes, pictures and audio transcriptions. Before, Scrivener I used to store these things in various folders on my computer.

Scrivener offered autosave and full-screen mode long before Apple and Microsoft made it to the party. Scrivener's cork board, outlining and collection modes provide users with various means of reviewing and laying out their documents.

It features a snapshot mode that allows you to roll back to previous versions of your draft, it syncs with Dropbox, and it handles notes and comments far more intuitively than any app I've used. It takes a few hours to learn, but the developers have created useful video tutorials and the members of Scrivener's forums are helpful.

Pages is Apple's answer to Word. It's pretty and intuitive if you use a Mac. However, Pages is not as useful or effective if you want to use the same document on a Windows machine, and don't get me started on Apple's insistence on the .PAGES proprietary format.

I know I can always export to a .DOC, .RFT or a .PDF, but it's an extra step I'd like to avoid. Saving your documents in iCloud works best if you have multiple Macs or iOS devices; it's a pain otherwise. For these reasons, Pages is best used if you are already tied into the Apple suite of products.

Google Docs: Google Drive is great for writers who travel, provided you are already using the G Suite. It features many of the features contained in Word and other desktop word processors. Google Docs may not be as fast or as polished as desktop applications, but Google makes collaboration and document sharing seamless.

Google Docs is free and you can use it almost anywhere, with the caveat that Google is hosting your Magnum Opus within Google Docs. Although I've used Google Docs in the past, I've been put off by the sometimes sluggish feel to the application when working on larger writing projects. That said, I once worked for a national radio station where the production team of a large show used Google Docs to share each day's running order and notes with each other.

A Plain .TXT Editor: Stripped down can be a good thing. Sometimes, I just want to type something really quickly without waiting for a word processor to open or worrying about a confusing range of options, menus, ribbons, templates, tables and tools. Plain text editors like Notepad (Windows) and TextEdit (OS X) are great because they're free, and they come pre-installed on their applicable operating systems.

These apps may lack lots of different formatting options and they can't handle tables and pictures but they are only meant for writing text. Also anyone on any device can open a .TXT file. They are backwards, forwards and every which way compatible. If you're in love with plain text, check out Notational Velocity for OS X. This application lets you organise your plain text files and it syncs with Simplenote.

Simplenote is a lightweight, free and easy to use tool for writers who want to take notes on the go. You can use Simplenote on your browser, mobile or desktop. There are also numerous third-party apps, and it plays nice with Dropbox. I previously relied on Simplenote to record ideas for blog posts.

IA Writer is a minimalist writing tool for OS X and iOS. It's great for writers working on shorter projects and for those who crave a distraction-free environment. IA Writer hides most of its options from users and focuses on the words on screen, meaning you're less likely to get distracted or confused by menus and preferences.

Grammarly/After the Deadline are spelling and grammar checkers. You can use them in your browser, via a WordPress plugin or as extensions for several writing applications. They check your writing for spelling and grammar errors, and tell you if your writing is hard to read or full of clichés and jargon. They are not a replacement for proofreading, but they are a last line of defence for writers.

Read my review of Grammarly.[3]

WordPress powers approximately a quarter of all websites today including my website www.becomeawritertoday.com. If you're serious about writing for the web, spend a couple of hours figuring out how WordPress works. Start by learning the differences between pages and posts.

Markdown is my favourite digital writing tool because it speeds up the process of writing and editing for the web. Invented by John Gruber in 2004, Markdown makes it easier to format text for the web. You can use special characters to pre-format links, lists, headings and various web styles, without having to type any HTML.

Then, you can convert Markdown to HTML using plugins like Jetpack for WordPress. Various word processors can also convert Markdown to HTML, which you can then paste into your content management system of choice. It takes about two hours to learn Markdown, but this investment will save you many hours manually formatting articles with HTML.

If you're interested in learning markdown, you can find the full syntax on daringfireball.net/projects/markdown.

Remember, don't put your search for the perfect writing tool in front of sitting down and writing. Just as the bad tradesman blames his tools when he can't finish a job, a bad writer blames their tools when they can't finish what they started.

---

3   http://becomeawritertoday.com/grammar-checker-review-grammarly/

16

EMBRACE STRUCTURE

"I fear those big words which make us so unhappy"
– James Joyce

DO YOU WANT to know how to organise your writing?

If you do, planning and structure are your new best friends.

You will find a writing project easier to finish, and readers will find it easier to consume your work if there's an underlying structure. This is why books have paragraphs, chapters and narrative arcs.

It's why blog posts have sub-headings and why newspaper articles are broken up with pull-out quotes, panels and boxes. Even the directors and writers of most successful films break them into three acts.

Planning and Structure for Productive Writers

Several years ago, I had to write a 20,000 plus word thesis about the literary works of the Irish author Christy Brown.

For months, I struggled with this thesis. I just couldn't get it to flow and I couldn't organise my ideas. I told my tutor I was afraid I wouldn't be able to finish my work. She said:

"Why don't you approach your thesis from a different angle? Why don't you outline it?"

I took my tutor's advice and worked out an outline of each section and chapter using pen and paper. I wrote down the title of each chapter on one hundred plus 6x4 index cards. Next, I wrote down points I wanted to cover within each chapter alongside various quotes, stories and other pieces of factual information. I laid my index cards out on large glass table, and I spent several hours reviewing them.

What happened next surprised me.

I was able to shift from one troublesome section or chapter to another easier one, without getting lost or stressed. I could see the overall structure of my thesis, even if it wasn't finished. In effect, I zoomed out from my thesis and moved the chapters and ideas around like the pieces on a chessboard.

I considered where I was repeating myself, what I was missing and what I needed to cover. Then, I sorted the index cards into piles that I wanted to keep, remove or combine. Next, I rewrote each of the index cards and I repeated this planning process.

I did this until I was left with a structure for my thesis that I could work with. Although the thesis changed during the course of writing and rewriting, this structure served as a light during the creative process that kept me from getting lost.

Reduce, Remove and Simplify

Confession: I hate shopping for clothes. It's time-consuming, draining and I'm terrible at it.

I never know what to buy and I always think there's a better choice just around the corner.

One hot summer's day, I had to buy a shirt and tie for a wedding. I spent several hours walking from suit shop to suit shop in Dublin and trying on clothes I didn't like. I was sweaty, tired and about to give up my search and go home. Then, I decided to try an airy and quiet shop near the bus stop.

When I walked inside, the owner took one look at me and pulled out a chair.

"You look like a man who needs a seat," he said. "How can I help you?"

I explained my predicament.

"I just don't know what I want," I said. "There's so much out there."

The owner of the suit shop asked what I liked and what I was looking for. Then, he laid out three shirts and three ties on the table for me to try on.

"Why only three?" I asked pointing to all the other suits and ties behind us.

"I never give a customer too much choice," he said. "It makes decisions harder."

He was right.

I found it much easier to pick from his three choices than the hundreds of other choices in the shop.

Why It Pays To Simplify Your Writing

The business writer and online entrepreneur, Chris Brogan best sums the benefits of simplification. He told the writer and podcaster James Altucher in a 2014 interview, "The sun can warm an entire field of daisies, or you can focus it such that it can burn through an inch of steel."

Focus on the heart of your writing and cut anything that doesn't add value. If you're struggling to simplify your writing, consider:

- What angles and points can you combine or remove?
- Are you being too technical?
- What should your writing focus on?
- What should it ignore?
- If an alien arrived from Mars and read your writing, would he or she understand it?
- Can you sum up your topic in one sentence?
- If not, what's preventing you from doing so?
- How can you use fewer words?

How I Simplify My Writing

When I'm writing feature articles, I reduce the number of interviewees I quote because I know too many interviewees can become confusing for the reader. This reduction also lends greater weight to the included interviewees, and it gives me room to analyse what they said.

While writing *A Handbook for the Productive Writer*, I simplified my work by reducing what I've discovered about productivity into 33 digestible strategies. I did this because I felt that 33 strategies was the best way of reducing my idea to the essentials.

When I'm writing a blog post, I pick an idea and consider people who will want to read about it. I ask what new perspective or information I can add to this topic and how I can solve a problem for readers. I make room for an introduction and conclusion and also for some factual information, personal anecdotes and stories from my commonplace book. Then, I write a rough first draft somewhere between 1000-1,500 words.

Later on, I re-read this first draft and consider what I should remove and rework. I check if my sentences are too long and if I can break up paragraphs into a list. I do this because online readers spend more time scanning than reading articles, and it's my job to make writing digestible for them.

Plan To Write, Plan To Finish

Authors like James Joyce and Samuel Beckett wrote without planning or structure, but even they learnt what structure was before they tore it away.

The next time you are faced with an intimidating writing project, break it into chunks that you can tackle one-by-one. On index cards, jot down words identifying these chunks, and then rearrange these in order of how your writing project unfolds.

This process will give you an early overview of your writing project. This planning will also help you zoom out and see all the pieces on your chessboard. From there, you can create a structure that works for you.

Your writing will evolve during the creative process, but having a plan and using structure can help you get from the blank page to the last page.

17

WRITE WITH A BEGINNER'S MIND

*"When you do something, you should burn yourself
completely, like a good bonfire, leaving no trace of yourself."*
– Shunryu Suzuki

So you're an expert.

You know how to organise your ideas, you've put in your 10,000 hours of dedicated practice, and you know how to write. But can you still write as if you are considering an idea for the first time?

Shunryu Suzuki was a Japanese Zen monk and teacher and the author of the book *Zen Mind, Beginner's Mind*. In his book of Zen teachings and talks, Suzuki writes that when we do something it should be without bias or preconceptions. Instead, when we do something it should consume us completely.

To take on a task and know how it will turn out beforehand is to hold something back from the creative fire. To bring your preconceptions and biases is to forget about the point of view of those who know less than you. Instead, put everything you know into the fire of the creative process and let it burn.

Perhaps the argument you set out to prove isn't as solid as you thought? Maybe a character in your story want to do something that you didn't expect? Or perhaps your research unearths a new angle or story for your work?

If you're an expert, this open-minded approach to writing is hard to take.

When you become practised at a task or skill, your writing voice dulls itself on a groove of repetition. Your arguments establish themselves and opinions solidify even before the fire of your hard work takes hold. You turn to the same haggard metaphors and imagery and drag them out long after their prime. You fail to see things from the point of view of your less informed readers. You miss those interesting detours and stops that form part of the creative process.

Because the beginner's eye belongs to your next, new reader.

The Unique Perspective of the Outsider

Consider starting a new job.

For the first few weeks or months, you are an outsider who sees the workplace differently to the rest of the team. Even if you keep your questions to yourself, you wonder why things are done one way and not the other. For those first few weeks, you are a unique commodity and sometimes forward-thinking managers will capitalise on your outsider's insight to make informed changes. They know you can see things the rest of the team can't.

When these first few weeks turn into months or even years, you will acquire expert knowledge about your company or workplace. You will become the kind of person who does things a certain way because that's how it's always been done.

You may have expert knowledge, experience and insight about a topic or field of study, but this can make you complacent.

How can you write something original when the tinder wood of your creativity is soaked with preconceptions? How many times have you made the same moot point? Have you become an insider?

If the facts change, abandon your arguments. Don't become too attached to any one idea or way of accomplishing things on the blank page. If you get the chance, leave your old arguments behind and don't look back.

Changing Your Mind (And Getting Away With It)

Writing with a beginner's mind means bringing a renewed sense of passion and curiosity to your project. It means asking and even answering questions you take for granted. It means accepting that your readers will know things that you don't and vice versa. It means seeing things with a beginner's eye.

Here's a little secret:

You can get away with changing your mind if you take readers on a journey with you. Readers love this. They'll forgive you for an about-turn if you explain the why and how of your about-turn.

At first, the Italian astronomer Galileo Galilei believed the world was flat like his scientific peers. Then in 1616, he presented his change of mind and argued why the world is round. Early in life, the British author George Orwell believed strongly in the entitlements of the upper class. Later in life, he satirised them in his dystopian novel *1984*.

The author Leo Tolstoy was a staunch follower of Russian Orthodox and a man who believed it was acceptable to keep serfs. Later in life, he explained why he had abandoned his old principles in his short book *A Confession*.

"I cannot recall those years without horror, loathing, and heart-rending pain. I killed people in war, challenged men to duels with the purpose of killing them, and lost at cards; I squandered the fruits of the peasants' toil and then had them executed; I was a fornicator and a cheat. Lying, stealing, promiscuity of every kind, drunkenness, violence, murder — there was not a crime I did not commit… Thus I lived for ten years."

You may not have committed a crime, duelled with your fellow man or lost at cards like Tolstoy but when you look back on the years past, what have you changed your mind about? Can you include this change of mind in your writing?

Burning Up With Your Reader

Hold out your hand for your reader and invite them on a journey that the two of you have never taken together. Show your reader why your idea warrants his or her attention. Reveal the mistakes you've made, the times you fell down, the lessons you learned and what your world looks like today.

Practice writing from this beginner's mind until you can approach the blank page without any preconceived notions. Write like you're experiencing something for the first time. Write like it's you and the reader against the world, and together you will burn like a good bonfire.

18

UNDERSTAND THE LIMITATIONS OF YOUR CRAFT

"Every person takes the limits of their own field of vision for the limits of the world." – Arthur Schopenhauer

DO YOU UNDERSTAND the limitations of the written word?

The written word only engages two to three of the five human senses: sight, touch, sound, taste and smell.

The reader can see your words on the page, but when you describe someone's face, the reader must use their imagination to fill the blanks. They can feel the weight and texture of the paper in their hands, but when you write about the texture of someone's skin, they will bring their biases to your writing. If you describe the bitter taste of a coffee, the reader's sense of taste and smell are just as likely to be triggered by the environment where they're reading your writing.

There are exceptions. Poetry read aloud is musical to the ear. You can also use onomatopoeia or words that sound like their meaning like cuckoo or sizzle to engage your reader's senses. Today, lots of writers also read their works to their readers at public readings or in the form of audio books.

The productive writer sometimes uses picture, video and audio to convey his or her message. He does this because he knows alternative media complements fine writing. He makes lengthy passages destined for the computer screen more digestible by breaking them up with bullet points, headings, stand-out quotes and the clever use of **bold** and *italics* formatting.

This is particularly true if you're writing for online readers who are just as likely to listen to an audio clip or watch as video as they are to read a blog post. For example, creating a presentation for SlideShare is a great way of combining carefully chosen words and sentences with high-quality pictures and exposing your ideas to a new audience.

Don't Stop Experimenting

Did you ever read my erotic fiction?

I'm embarrassed to tell you this but several years ago, I researched what was popular and trending, and I tried to write several different erotic short stories. I discovered erotic fiction is exceptionally difficult to write without coming across as clichéd or sleazy. My stories came across as both.

I never published my stories, and I discovered I don't have the talent or desire to write the next *Fifty Shades Of Grey*. Thankfully, my humiliation was a private one, an experiment that helped me find the limitations of my craft.

The best way to discover the limitations of your craft is to explore what works and doesn't work for you, what excites you and what bores you. Do this by taking on new creative and writing challenges. Through brave experimentation, you will figure out the rules of writing and discover the ones that are OK to bend and the ones you should snap in half.

If writers didn't take time to experiment with their craft, we wouldn't have books like *Ulysses* or *The Dubliners*. James Joyce is an extreme example (him being a genius and all), but aspiring writers can learn from the working habits of the greats.

For you, this may mean writing poetry, a novel, a short story or a personal essay. It means getting out of your creative comfort zone.

If you've written a story in the first person, rewrite it in the third person. If you've written a blog post about the benefits of meditation, turn it into 50 reasons why meditation is better than sex. If you've just finished an article, remove the introduction and insert the conclusion in its place. If you opened your article with a statistic, use a quote or even a statement that will rile up your reader. If you tried to be impartial, rewrite your work using a strong and personal point of view.

Experimenting with your writing is time-consuming, and you're going to make mistakes, but nobody has to see them and the more you make, the better a writer you will become. It is a great way of developing your writing voice and pushing your boundaries beyond what you feel most comfortable doing

At the very least, experimenting means you are less likely to become bored with your craft and more excited about the possibilities of the blank page. If you don't find writing enjoyable, then what's the point?

What People See Vs. What You Do

The iceberg is a remarkable feat of nature. The largest ever Arctic iceberg was discovered in 1882 near Baffin Island. This iceberg was 13km long by 6km wide, and it towered 20 metres above the waterline. I find these formations remarkable because only 10 percent of an iceberg is visible above the waterline, while the other 90 percent lies beneath the water.

The work you share, the writing people read, this is your 10 percent that we can see. The hard work, the mistakes, the failed experiments, the grind and the torn-up manuscripts; these activities make up the 90 percent of what lies beneath the water, what really goes on in the life of a productive writer.

19

BUILD YOUR PLATFORM

*"Compared to the cost of renting eyeballs,
buying a platform is cheap."* – Seth Godin

IF YOU'RE SERIOUS about writing, you need a platform to tell stories about yourself, to showcase your work and to find readers.

Today productive writers build their platforms online. Paulo Coelho has an astonishing ten million followers on Twitter (@ paulocoelho). Neil Gaiman is also an avid user of Twitter and blogs at journal.neilgaiman.com. George RR Martin also blogs about his work on www.georgemartin.com. James Altucher writes about creativity, self-publishing and business, amongst other things on his blog. Jeff Goins is another popular non-fiction writer who uses his blog and social media to communicate with his audience.

The gatekeepers between you and your audience no longer exist. You can use the internet to create opportunities that weren't available when writers like John Cheever, Virginia Woolf and Stephen King started out. You can start a blog, develop a professional, social media presence within your niche, self-publish on Amazon, give away short books for free on your website and even seek out other writers online and learn from them.

If you do this, you will start to get the real-world feedback you need to improve your writing, and this feedback will encourage you to keep on going when you want to stop.

Building your platform gives you more opportunities to communicate with your audience and find out what they want. A blog is the perfect platform for anyone who wants to write and practice finishing what they started.

There, you can experiment with various writing styles, explore your niche and build an audience. It also gets you into the habit presenting your work to more than just your wife or husband, family member or best friend. It gets you into the habit of finishing.

If people dislike your writing, celebrate. They're reading your work. And isn't this the goal? You can still use this free feedback to develop a thicker skin (an essential trait for any writer) and improve your craft.

Even if no one reads your blog, it gets you into the habit of writing every day and, for most aspiring writers, that's a great habit to cultivate. Spending time on social media channels like Twitter, Facebook and Google+ isn't a replacement for writing. You can use social media to interact with the wider community, but don't let these channels distract you from the blank page.

Unless you're Paulo Coelho.

Then you can do whatever the hell you want.

Show It Some Respect

Your platform deserves your respect.

If you are writing a blog, you have to write for a digitally literate audience. Include multimedia content, link to pre-existing and external content, and end your posts with a call-to-action that engages readers.

If you are writing a report, this platform demands you provide supporting evidence that you can cite to back up your findings or conclusions. If you don't do this, your report will have no authority.

If you are writing for a magazine or newspaper, you have to respect the tone of voice and messaging style of the publication you are writing for. You could interview experts the readers of this publication are interested in hearing from. Or you could follow up on a theme that the magazine addressed previously.

If you are writing content for a social media campaign, your platform(s) demand that you be concise, entertaining and personable. Some engaging visuals won't hurt either. Fail to do this and your followers won't click, share and engage.

And, if you are writing copy for a website, your copy should link to pre-existing articles on your website and provide visitors with information relevant to their search queries.

Respecting your platform means knowing when to use a formal tone of voice, when to describe how something affected you and if you should reinforce a point by saying something is shit or shit hot.

As a journalist, I wrote for tabloids and broadsheets. I found broadsheet articles required a lot more planning and research than tabloids. I also found the tabloid platform to be more restrictive than a broadsheet as, although the language of a tabloid is emotional, it's difficult to convey a meaningful point using concise, everyday language.

If you're going to build a platform for your writing, here are some simple but effective tips that I learnt from several years of blogging:

Own Your Website and Domain Name:

When you're creating a website for your writing, buy a website domain name and hosting package that you have complete control over. Then, build and manage your site using a tool like WordPress. Don't pay for any of those website builder offerings with a monthly subscription. They work out more expensive in the long run, and these service can change your domain name if you stop paying them. Remember, if you don't completely own your domain, you're not in charge of your writing or your platform.

Control How Much Time You Spend on Social Media

To some people this is sacrilege, but unless social media is your business, it's a side-attraction.

You can use social media to promote your work, to engage with readers and to research your market. However, if you're doing this at the expense of writing and finishing what you are working on, then you are wasting valuable time.

Spend your time writing, and afterwards approach social media as a way of amplifying existing content and as a free market research tool.

Build Your Home Base

Social media is a good way of interacting with readers, but you should make a point of directing your followers from social media onto your website or mailing list. Amazon, Facebook and Twitter are outposts that you have less control over. When they change the rules (as they often do), there's little you can do.

On your website, on the other hand, you're in charge. It's your home base, and it should be the number one place where readers and customers can find you. This is another reason why it's so important that you have *complete control* over your domain and hosting.

Grow Your Email List

Your email list enables you to communicate directly with readers or customers. After you've set up a mailing list make a point to contact people on your list regularly, i.e. don't let your list grow stale.

This kind of reader engagement makes marketing your writing easier, and you can even ask your loyal fans or readers for feedback and advice about your writing. Plus, you will be less dependent on search engines and social media for traffic and readers.

Give Your Readers What They Want

This will turn them into loyal fans that are more likely to open their wallets when the time comes. For example, I wrote an ebook about Twitter that I gave away on my website. Even though it took over thirty hours to research and write, I gave it away for free.

The sole purpose of this ebook is to win over people onto my email list. And this strategy works; new people join my mailing list every day.

My strategy is hardly an original strategy. Most high-profile blogs offer free valuable content. Even Amazon gives away free ebooks and provides readers with samples of books they want to buy.

If you're a writer who wants to market your writing, your goal should be to get them in the door. You can earn money later on.

Don't Obsess about Design or Search Engine Optimisation

Unless design and SEO are your areas of expertise, pay for and outsource whatever you can. Your job is to write or to create high-value articles that your customers love. Everything else is secondary. Instead, buy a professional, premium theme for your WordPress powered website.

This way you won't have to worry as much about design or SEO. If you're looking for a list of tools that can help you build a more effective blog, please read this post I wrote about blogging tools and software that I recommend.

Spending time on the finer points of SEO and tweaking your design won't help you finish whatever you're writing or working on.

Your Website Isn't For Hard Sales

Instead of filling your website with ads for third-party products and services, save this space for your writing and your products. If you force your books, writing or other offerings down your readers' throats, this will give your readers a reason to leave. Give them a reason to love you; make 'em feel something.

For example, the business writer Pat Flynn writes about how he earns money online at smartpassiveincome.com. Flynn makes a point to avoid selling directly to people on his mailing list. He also avoids hard-sales on his website, and instead he prioritises providing valuable content for his readers. Flynn still makes a significant amount of money each month because his readers trust him, and they buy products that *he* uses or products that *he* created.

"You won't get any hard sells from me, long sales pages or fluffed up stuff – just real life case studies and recommendations based on my own experience with online business and blogging," Flynn writes.

Make a Plan for Publishing Your Writing (And Stick to It)

If you're going to blog, make a plan for publishing a new blog post every day, week or month. It doesn't matter how often so long as you stick to your publishing schedule, and don't abandon your website altogether. This way, you will get into the habit of starting and finishing writing projects, and your readers will come to expect and even look forward to your writing.

How To Market Your Platform

Let me tell you about David.

He's a professional writer (blogger, fiction writer, non-fiction writer, etc.) who doesn't like marketing his work. He says his job is to write, not to promote, and that if he works hard enough on his art, then his readers will come.

There's just one problem.

Only a few people have come across David's work. And when they do, they don't stay long.

Does any of this sound familiar?

Not too long ago, I was David. And if you're a writer struggling to find an audience for your work online, he's you too.

Writing is a hard, demanding craft, and there's nothing more disappointing than releasing your work into a vacuum. The good news is you can overcome all of these problems.

Research What Your Readers Want

Social media is a resource that marketers love because they can survey what their audience wants and develop personas.

You should view social media as a tool for researching what your ideal readers want and to test how they will receive your work. You can also use social media to find writers or publishers who can help your career.

With tools like BuzzSumo, you can use social media to research your current writing project.

For example, when I type the term "marketing writing" into BuzzSumo, I can see most shared articles with this keyword or about this topic across social media.

This enables me to research popular blog posts and articles, find other writers I should work with or follow, and create a hit list of websites I want to write for

Similarly, if you've finished a new book or giveaway for your blog, you could A/B test the title or cover by running a free poll on Facebook or Google+. These types of polls helped me pick a more relevant cover and title for my book.

Finally, before you publish your next article, take five minutes to find and review what's already out there and what your audience has shared. Then, share what you've created with this audience using a time-saving app like Buffer or HootSuite.

If you don't believe that writers should use social media, check out what Paulo Coelho is doing. Or Neil Gaiman. Or Stephen King.

Email Your Readers

Email marketing is a traditional digital marketing strategy, but it's one that forward-looking writers should feel at home with.

Think of your emails as a letter between you and your reader.

There's a long tradition of this. Harper Lee, Roald Dahl and C.S. Lewis are just three of the many authors who wrote letters to their fans.

Through email, you can tell readers about your best work, explain your ideas, ask for feedback and gather information that will help you improve your next book, blog post or article.

It takes several hours to write an auto-responder email campaign, but once you set this campaign up, it will direct new readers to your best work for as long as it's active.

Meanwhile, you can concentrate on writing new articles, essays or books safe in the knowledge that your blog – and by extension your writing – is marketing itself.

Tip: Give members of your email list high-quality bonus articles for free such as chapters of your book, worksheets or templates that they can use. This way, your most loyal readers will get more value from your work.

Write Guest Blog Posts

You're a forward-looking writer committed to the art of blogging. You know how important it is to have a digital presence, and that blogging helps you practice your craft.

Writing guest blog posts for high-profile websites is a great way to market your writing. When you write for a large website, your words will appear in front of a new audience that is unfamiliar with your work.

You can make peace with this marketing strategy because it allows you to keep writing and promote your work.

Every writer who wants to improve knows how important critical feedback is. When an editor of the website you're writing for reviews your posts, you will receive feedback that will help you improve as a writer. This constructive feedback is something aspiring writers pay for – but you can get it for free through guest posting.

Finally, if you write several successful guest blog posts, you can ask the site owners to share your writing or promote your book. This is cheaper and more efficient than trying to run an advertising campaign.

Tip: When your guest blog post goes live, write a second blog post on your website that links to the guest blog post. This should expand on the guest post or welcome new readers to your website. This way, your blog keeps up to date and your existing readers will read your guest posts.

Your Guide to Writing Great Guest Posts

Before I wrote my first guest post, I resented the idea of spending precious time and energy writing something and then giving this to someone else.

Surely I was better off writing posts and publishing them on my site?

I was dead wrong.

There are a couple of reasons.

Firstly, my personal blogging mentor Jon Morrow told me writing guest posts for large websites is the writer's equivalent of opening for the Rolling Stones when you're an up and coming band in search of new fans. It's the quickest way to grow your audience.

Here's the thing:

If you perform your job as a guest writer, some of this site's audience will visit your website, join your email list and read your writing.

Writing guest posts also gives you free access the quality editorial feedback that you need to improve as a writer. The editors of larger websites are trained professionals, and they can help you unearth problems in your writing that you otherwise would have to pay a tutor lots of money for.

I don't know about you but most new writers I know don't have lots of money many to hire a personal and expensive editor. This leaves one other option:

Writing guest posts.

If Charles Bukowski Gave His Best Stuff Away So Can You

Charles Bukowski was one of America's most famous poets and novelists.

In his famous collection of Poetry *The Pleasures of the Damned*, Bukowski complained his heroes (Hemingway, Scott F. Fitzgerald) were able to find an audience for their work easier in the 1920s than he could in the 1940s and 1950s:

"It was much easier to be a genius in the twenties, there were only 3 or 4 literary magazines…. you could possibly meet Picasso for a glass of wine."

Then, Bukowski bemoaned the amount of publications he had to deal with (i.e. write for) to build his audience in 1951:

Now there are so many of us, hundreds of literary magazines, hundreds of presses, thousands of titles.

Bukowski would have just loved the millions of websites, blogs and publications today's writers contend with.

If Bukowski can do it, so you can you.

Now, let's explode some of the most popular myths about writing guest posts.

Myth: It's Your Editor's Job to Write the Headline

The headline is the most important part of any article or blog post.

It's the first thing your readers see and if it's written well, your headline will convince readers to click on a link to your article.

When you're pitching an editor, include a strong headline following the style of the blog in question.

Often this is enough to convince an editor to read your post.

You can write a strong headline by studying headlines of the five most popular blog posts on the site you're pitching.

Alternatively, you can make your writing life easier by studying the covers of popular magazines like *Cosmo* or *Esquire*, and then emulating what they do.

These headline writers are highly-paid professionals that you can learn from for free.

Here's how this works:

1. Type *Cosmo* into Google image search

2. Pick a magazine cover and write down 5-10 headlines

3. Adapt each headline idea around your topic

Myth: One Idea Is Enough To Woo Your Editor

If you include one idea, your chances of getting published depend solely on the merits of your single idea.

If you include two ideas, your editor has a dilemma.

If you include three ideas, your editor has options.

You don't need to go into great detail for each idea (and a time-strapped editor with a thousand emails to read won't thank you for a 1,000-word email), but give your editor more than what they're expecting.

Myth: You Can Take as Much Time as You Want to Write Your Post

I was a professional journalist for several years, and I can tell you professional writers look for deadlines and stick to them.

If your guest post is accepted, it's good practice to either ask your editor for a deadline or submit a completed post within one to two weeks.

Worried you can't do this?

Make life easier on yourself by writing a rough draft of your article before you pitch the editor in question.

This way you can rework your draft before submitting it.

But what if your post is rejected?

Don't worry.

You can still rework the idea for another website or if that fails, you can use the post on your blog.

Myth: The Guest Posting Guidelines Are for Fools

The guest post guidelines differ from site to site, and woe betide the writer who ignores them.

They may ask you to do things like:

- Hit a target word count
- Include an image for your post
- Link to other articles or influencers in your post
- Write a linking post on your website
- Email an editor rather than the site owner (more on this in a moment)

One site I pitched hid a 'password' in the middle of their guest posting guidelines and asked that serious writers (i.e. the ones who read the guidelines) include this password in their initial email.

You can typically find the writing guidelines on the About page, the contact page or on another dedicated page on the site in question.

Myth: There's No Need To Spend Time Building Relationships Before You Make Your Pitch

I sometimes comment on popular posts on the sites I want to write for multiple times before making a pitch.

Commenting on the popular and new blog posts will help you develop a relationship with the site owner or the editor in question.

I also share these posts multiple times using Twitter because Twitter notifies the site owners that I shared their posts. This notification makes it easier for me to build a relationship with the site in question (who doesn't like their writing being shared?) and get a response to my guest post pitch.

Another guest blogging tactic is to link to various posts on the target website on your blog. This tactic is more successful if you are targeting mid-level rather than top-level blogs. The former may not have that many links (and will notice yours) whereas the latter will have thousands.

Myth: It Doesn't Matter What the Editor's Name Is

In his book *How to Win Friends and Influence People,* — Dale Carnegie writes:

"Names are the sweetest and most important sound in any language."

Most larger websites employ a full-time editor who manages content on behalf of the site owner.

As a writer, it's your job to find out the name of this editor.

Whatever you do, don't start your email by saying 'hi' and then moving into your pitch. This will make your email sound cold and impersonal. The guest posting guidelines of most sites often include the names of the editors in question.

Alternatively if you're stuck, address the site owner by name.

Myth: Didn't Hear Back Immediately? Move On

The owners and editors of popular websites are busy people with even busier inboxes.

If they don't respond to your initial guest post pitch immediately, don't take it personally. Instead, seven days after you make your pitch, send a follow up email politely asking if they received your submission.

A week is long enough to avoid harassing the editor but not so long that they forget about you.In the majority of cases, the editor will respond to the follow-up submission.

Four of five of my pitches received a response after I took this approach. If they don't, you can try again in one week or take your idea to another website.

The web is a big place.

Myth: Your Job is Over When Your Post Goes Live

Professional writers are always thinking about the next job; you should too.

When you write a guest post for a popular, website thank everybody that shares or comments on your posts and respond to their comments.

If you have time, read the bios of those who share your posts on Twitter.

If these people have a relationships with a site that you want to write for, contact them immediately with a new guest post idea.

You will be fresh in their mind, and they will be receptive to your ideas for their site. A few days after your post is published, send the editor a short email thanking them for the opportunity.

This way, you can keep the door open for future submissions. Even if you decide not to write for them again, this will leave a positive impression with the editor.

Here's the thing:

Leaving a positive impression is the hallmark of a professional writer.

Winning New Readers and Influencing Your Audience

Friendship is a long-term game, and so is writing guest posts.

Yes, it takes some time to get started if you haven't written a guest post before.

However after you've written several guest posts, the editors of larger and more popular websites will become more receptive to your ideas because you have a body of work, which you can point to.

Plus you can use your old posts to build your credibility as a writer with your expanding audience on your blog or website.

Now go give your best work away for free.

If anyone asks, tell them Charles Bukowski sent you.

But I'm a Writer, Not a Marketer!

Can I blunt?

This is a cop-out, and it's one I spent years making.

I've sat in writing groups and listened to myself and my peers describe how marketing a book or a piece of writing is debasing. At the time, I agreed with the other members of this group that marketing should be left to the marketers and writing to the writers.

We were wrong.

You may be a writer and your books, blog posts and articles may be art, but what's the point if nobody finds your work?

In his book *All Marketers Are Liars*, the oracle of online marketing Seth Godin provides numerous examples of companies, brands and business people that tell authentic stories about their products.

He writes, "When you find a story that works, live that story, make it true, authentic, and subject to scrutiny. All marketers are storytellers."

Did I mention Godin has written 17 books?

Don't feel bad or sleazy about these kinds of marketing activities.

Instead, you are telling stories about your work. These are stories that you may know well, but which your future readers haven't heard yet.

As a writer, your most important task for the day is to cultivate your writing routine and create. After all, you can't market your work if you haven't produced anything of value. However, your job doesn't end when you press submit, upload your new eBook to Amazon or send your writing to your editor.

Research what your audience wants, build relationships with thought leaders who can help and keep searching for ways to get in front of new audiences. This is what the productive writer does. He or she does it because they know committing to publishing and sharing their work publicly gives them the momentum they need to keep on going, to keep on writing.

20

EXERCISE LIKE YOUR CRAFT
DEPENDS ON IT

"Exerting yourself to the fullest within your individual limits: that's the essence of running, and a metaphor for life— and for me, for writing as well. I believe many runners would agree." – Haruki Murakami

PHYSICAL EXERCISE IS a worthy and important pursuit for the productive writer.

Haruki Murakami, the Japanese author of books like *Kafka on the Shore* and *After Dark*, says running and cycling helps him become more creative. When he's working on a novel, and after his work is complete for the day, Murakami swims for 1500 metres or runs 10 kilometres. This is something Murakami does almost every day.

"For me, the main goal of exercising is to maintain, and improve, my physical condition in order to keep on writing novels," he writes.

Any writer struggling to finish a project can learn from Murakami's approach.

Writing involves working hard on a single task at length, as do intense physical activities like swimming, cycling, football and so on. It takes focus, concentration and discipline to succeed at these intense physical activities, just as it does on the blank page.

The scientists are on Murakami's side too.

According to Michael Mumford of the University of Oklahoma, 30 minutes of aerobic exercise will help you become more creative.

When I'm stuck on a troublesome piece, I sometimes go for a run, a swim or even a long walk. I'm not going to lie and saying exercising is always easy and enjoyable, but it does help me cultivate discipline, and it helps me focus. There, in the pool or on the road, when I'm not thinking about writing at all, a solution arises, and I see a way through whatever problem I'm facing.

Thirty minutes of exercise a day isn't too much, especially if you're pursuing a craft that requires you to sit down for hours at a time. Exercising will give you more energy, a break, and a new perspective on your work.

Meditation for Writers

Meditation, like exercise, can help you write too. Meditation and writing have a lot in common; they both involve sitting in one place and focusing on one task for extended periods of time. It one of the best ways to spark creativity, improve focus and make you smarter.

There are dozens of high-profile studies that demonstrate the links between meditation, creativity and focus.

For example, a 2012 scientific study by the Leiden University in the Netherlands found that "…meditation leads to better performance in a distributed-attention task and reinforces the view that meditation practice can have a lasting and generalizable impact on human cognition."

Sitting quietly on a cushion and focusing on your breath for just fifteen minutes each day makes it easier to sit in front of a computer or the blank page and write for extended periods. Meditation also serves as a necessary and welcome break from a computer screen or a troublesome sentence.

Meditation won't solve your physical problems directly, but it will help you become more aware of the times you need to take a break. And it can help writers become more accepting of chronic pain.

The next time you're in a creative rut, put on a pair of runners or meditate on it.

Why Physical Health Is Crucial For Productive Writers

Writing looks like an easy enough activity.

To the untrained observer, it's just one man or woman sitting on a comfortable chair, plucking words from a dictionary and spinning an indulgent yarn.

For most writers, the craft of producing prose is anything but easy or magical.

Writing requires a certain degree of physical and mental endurance and focus. A writer has to sit in one spot for hours every day and sustain their concentration for extended periods. And, they have do so alone without the distraction or encouragement of office colleagues or the material world.

A writer must have enough energy to sit and focus without becoming too distracted or tired to write. This kind of work is mentally exhausting. Physically, it can take its toll too.

Some days when I write for an extended period, my back aches, my eyes dry up, my hands cramp and my head spins. And when I close my eyes, all I can see is floating black and white dots. Last year, I spent several weeks attending physiotherapy sessions for sciatica. I experienced sciatica because I was spending too much time sitting down.

You can overcome physical complaints like these by taking short but regular breaks from the screen or the blank page and by exercising when you're not writing. The physio gave me a number of exercises to do and even suggested that I do certain things (like reading my work) while standing up.

If you are in pain for another reason, say because of an illness, it will become much harder to craft a meaningful sentence.

How can you write while you head throbs?

If you are particularly stressed, angry or emotional, it's difficult to achieve the kind of focus necessary for extended periods of examination and good writing.

Contrary to popular belief, hangovers don't make for effective prose. It may be entertaining to read about a drunken night out, but it's almost always impossible to write under the influence while hungover.

Even Ernest Hemingway and Scott F. Fitzgerald attempted to write sober towards the end of their writing careers because they recognised being wildly intoxicated doesn't always make for wildly intoxicating prose or productive writing.

"First you take a drink, then the drink takes a drink, then the drink takes you," Fitzgerald said.

Yes, Writing Is Sometimes Painful

I'm talking about the deep introspective writing that real writers put themselves through.

Writing should almost never be physically painful. It's not good practice to write when you're in pain, and there's no sense in suffering through your practice or making your health worse.

My physical therapist provided me with an assessment and a series of exercises.

I found paying a professional more beneficial than diagnosing myself by reading articles online then and treating myself by watching YouTube videos.

There are times when it's worth getting the opinion of an expert.

If you need outside help to overcome physical pain while writing, get it.

21

CONSERVE YOUR WILLPOWER

"The life of the professional writer – like that of any freelance, whether she be a plumber or a podiatrist – is predicated on willpower." – Will Self

'I just can't be bothered.' 'I'm just too tired.' 'I don't have the energy today.'

Have you ever made these types of excuses when it's time to write?

If you have, don't beat yourself up. This form of procrastination is natural.

In a 2009 study, Roy Baumeister, a psychologist at Florida State University, carried out an experiment whereby he asked students to sit next to a plate of fresh-baked chocolate-chip cookies. He gave permission to some students to eat the cookies, and he told others to avoid eating any of the treats. Afterward, Baumeister gave both groups difficult puzzles to solve.

The students who'd resisted eating the cookies found these puzzles more difficult to complete, and they abandoned the task. Their mental resources were depleted. On the other hand, those students who ate the cookies worked on the puzzles for longer. Baumeister found they were able to focus for longer because they had more mental resources.

If you're working on a difficult writing project, your productivity will suffer if your willpower is running low and you will become more likely to experience a creative drought.

Consider:

- Have you ever planned to write at the end of the day, only to come home exhausted and watch television instead?
- Do you find your word counts are lower when you write while tired?
- Do you find it difficult to concentrate on writing projects after a stressful event or a busy morning?

If you answered yes to these questions, then your writing was affected by a lack of willpower. The good news is it's easy to conserve your willpower and avoid a creative drought.

How to Conserve Your Willpower

Set yourself up for success the day before you get to work. At the end of your day, prepare the next day's writing in advance. Decide what you are going to work on or write about and for how long. You could even go as far as tidying your workspace, arranging your notes and opening up the writing application on your computer.

The next morning when you wake up and get to your desk, you won't have to make any decisions about your writing, and you won't have to waste time getting your tools or your project ready. All you have to do is sit down and do the work.

Another way to conserve your willpower is to decide on your most important tasks for the following day beforehand. This is an approach productive people use to accomplish more in the workplace. At the end of the day, spend five minutes writing down three to five tasks that you want to accomplish the next day.

For example, you could decide to free write, edit and then market an article in that order. Alternatively, you could decide to brainstorm, proofread and research a chapter of your new book or you could write down what you're going to do once you finish writing for the day. The idea here is that you won't waste mental energy the following morning figuring out what you need to do and when. You will just get up and get to it.

Your Priorities and Their Priorities

Deciding on your most important tasks each day forces you to review your commitments in advance. These regular mini-reviews will give you a chance to check in with how your writing is progressing. And they will get you into the habit of identifying and overcoming hurdles preventing you from finishing what you started.

The next day when you start work, progress through your most important tasks in order and first thing. The key is to finish these tasks before you check email, make phone calls, arrange meetings or meet with colleagues, before you attend to things that pop up. The majority of these other activities are items on someone else's To Do list. Yes, they may be important, but are they as important as your writing?

Remember, every time you say yes to someone else's priorities, you're saying no to your writing. Sometimes, being successful means being a little selfish.

You can also conserve and replenish your willpower by looking after yourself. You can do this by sleeping, eating healthily, exercising, meditating, doing the right thing at the right times, taking naps and even by listening to music.

Me? I like writing first thing in the morning because it sets up the entire day. It makes me feel like the entire day is golden because I put some words down onto the page, however ugly. If a meeting runs over, if there's a last minute appointment or a crisis with a colleague, it doesn't derail my day.

Your Best Self

Conserve your willpower for the moments when you really need it, for when it's time to write, to create, to live. If you cultivate this habit, it will become easier and more natural to write every day and you will gain the momentum you need to keep going even when you want to stop.

22

START A FIGHT

"After all, the ultimate goal of all research is not objectivity, but truth." – Helene Deutsch

DITCH ANY NOTIONS you have about being an objective writer.

Take a stance.

Objectivity is a falsehood, and objective writing is a style of writing best left to serious journalists and scientists. Even then, the most seasoned journalists and scientific writers bring a natural level of subconscious bias to their writings. They can only write through the frame of their upbringing, education and years of experience as a journalist or scientific writer. They can only see things through their gaze; everything else is second-hand information.

Yes, there are times when a writer should avoid inserting himself or herself directly into the piece they are working on, for example, a journalist writing about a natural disaster. Yes, there are times when a writer should give information rather than straight up opinion, for example, a scientist writing about a serious medical condition.

Most of the time though, this type of writing is boring and unnecessary. Almost nobody will read it.

When you write, take a stance. Have an opinion and pick a fight. Call another writer or an expert in your field out. Tell readers what you believe. Argue for or against prevailing thinking. Explain your passion or what you've learnt. Even if the material you're working with is boring and grey, make it your job to inject some colour.

You can take a stance by writing from the heart, or you can use calculated reasoning. Whatever your approach, there's nothing less invigorating than an author who is planted undecidedly in the middle.

If you succeed, you will invoke a reaction in your readers. They may hate what you're saying or disagree with you entirely, but at least they're engaging with you.

Just remember that having a stance doesn't mean being vicious or nasty for the sake of it.

The Case for the Modest Writer

Some readers will know less than you do, others will know more. Some will be interested in what you have to say, some will think you're wrong, and others just won't care.

Writers who try to impress readers with how much they know or how clever they are almost always flat on their faces. Those who hold back on the page for fear of embarrassment or because of foolish pride will produce a mediocre piece of work that will be forgotten.

If you want to avoid these pitfalls, reveal your weaknesses or faults. Let your readers know where you went wrong and how you're trying to improve (if at all).

It's OK to admit that you don't know everything and that you made mistakes. These kinds of intimate details make it far easier for readers to relate to you.

I admit there are times when a writer doesn't need to put their personality in the centre of the blank page. For example, if what you are writing is hard news or cold scientific analysis, present the facts rather than the man.

Readers love brutal honesty because they've made mistakes too. Readers are not some homogenous group of people who judge your work as one. They're individuals who make mistakes, and they want to hear about yours.

Even if you're writing a more formal article, such as a step-by-step guide or a tutorial, it's almost always a good idea to ask readers if they have any questions or suggestions at the end of your article. The best formal articles encourage discussion, debate or feedback.

I've tried to include as many practical writing tips as I could find and think of in this book, but I also accept that some more accomplished writers may have ideas I've yet to consider.

That's OK with me because, through writing, I'm seeking to learn more about the craft of writing and share the learnings of my journey with you.

Don't you want to do the same?

The Case for Common Human Decency

Somewhere, someone on the internet is wrong.

Is that person you?

Are you hiding behind your computer screen?

Have you ever ranted or told someone that their work is terrible and why they should never create again?

I'm being unfair – you strike me as an honest reader – but if you read the comments on popular YouTube videos, the reviews of books on Amazon, or the comments on a popular forum post, you can find hundreds of examples of people who don't demonstrate common human decency. They may be shouting in CAPs, telling the creator that they are wrong, that their work is shit, that they've failed themselves and let down their family down.

I've a confession to make.

Years ago, I was a little like that. I reviewed films for a local newspaper. The newspaper didn't have a budget to send reviewers to the films, so I made up my reviews.

I wanted to make a name for myself, so I analysed and criticised the hard work of other creative professionals even though I hadn't watched their accomplishments or failures. It was an awful way to spend my time, and my reviews were terrible.

My editor was OK about it, but I lost my self-respect as a writer.

I learnt it's easier to attack someone's work for its obvious flaws than it is to take the time to leave your comfort zone, create something and put yourself out there by sharing your ugly bastard child with the world.

These days I only ever take the time to write about something I like, use or am passionate about.

The act of writing is a gift that writers can use to bring light into dark places. Even abrasive writers like Charles Bukowski were more concerned with their failings than the failings of others.

"If you're losing your soul and you know it, then you've still got a soul left to lose," Bukowski said.

Today, I've a lot of respect for established reviewers and critics like the recently deceased American film critic Roger Ebert. The best critics value the creative arts, they're honest, and they engage with their readers.

If it's your job to respond to or critique other people's work, look for the higher ground. If the work you are reviewing is badly written, write a *constructive* critique. Explain the negatives and the positives to someone's work. Or provide a personal context that helps the reader understand if the work in question is worth their time or money.

If work in question is ill-judged, explain why without humiliating the person on the other end. If this isn't possible, either don't write anything or think of a time when you wrote something that failed.

The productive writer – hell any writer – has failed at some point. All of us should appreciate how difficult it is to create.

23

———

TELL A LIE

"Fiction is the lie that tells the truth, after all." – Neil Gaiman

DO YOU ENJOY telling lies? Do you have a little something on the side? Are you cheating?

If want your writing to sparkle, you should. New writers sometimes feel paralysed because they are not an expert in their chosen topic or because they just can't think of a good or original idea. After browsing Amazon or the shelves in a local bookstore, it feels like everything has been said, the best books are already published, and there are no good ideas left.

There are, but you've just got to fake it until you find one.

More experienced writers sometimes say they want to publish more of their work and more frequently, but they often feel hamstrung by deadlines and other professional commitments.

If you're having these types of creative problems, you've got to tell yourself a little white lie.

You've got to cheat.

You've got to have a little something on the side.

Why Telling a White Lie Is the Gentle Shove You Need

When I first started researching *A Handbook for the Productive Writer*, I lied to myself.

Even though there are lots of great productivity books, I told myself I could find something original to say. I told myself I could offer up a fresh insight into the world of productivity. The sad reality was that when I started this book, I didn't have any good ideas or fresh insights, but then a funny thing happened.

This white lie gave me enough momentum to start writing my book.

When I started writing my book, I began to apply what I discovered about productivity to the art of writing. Through doing this, I discovered a different perspective on both topics. Telling a lie to myself or faking it helped me finish writing my book.

Here's the good news:

There's a scientific merit to telling yourself white lies.

According to Dr. Paul Seager, a British psychology lecturer, it's healthy to tell white lies:

"To keep society running smoothly, we need to tell white lies. If your partner comes home with their latest piece of artwork and says, 'What do you think of this?', it shows they want support. Whether you like it or not, you're going to say it's nice."

Like the supporting partner, why not support your ideas and your work?

Tell yourself you have something original to say even if you don't. Later on, you'll find out that you do have something original to say after all. And if you're worried you've deluded yourself, you can always sense-check your ideas with the help of your editor, your writing group and anyone who reads early versions of your work.

How Telling a White Lie Can Freshen Up Your Writing

You can use a white lie to freshen up the way you write about an old topic.

For example, various social media experts claim Facebook is the perfect social media network for business people who want to talk to customers or in our case writers who want to talk to their readers. They cite Facebook's 500 million plus users, its ease of use, and its vast data points.

Let's assume these experts are wrong.

Let's tell a white lie to ourselves and say Facebook is the worst social media network for writers who want to talk to customers or readers.

Using this little lie, you write an article that calls on all forwarding-thinking writers to abandon Facebook. Tell them to try Twitter, Instagram or Pinterest and explain how they can get started. You can do this by writing about what happened when you took this approach. Or you could argue that writers should forget about social media and concentrate on building their email list instead.

Then you could give your article a headline like:

Forget Facebook: Your Email List is King

Or

What Facebook Isn't Telling You: What Smart Writers Need to Know

I'm not suggesting you wilfully mislead your reader. Instead, the productive writer sometimes turns a fact on its head and attacks their project from a new and exciting angle. They look for a way in that their peers haven't thought of. Don't believe me? Writers use this trick all the time.

How often have you clicked on articles with headlines like:

- Everything you know about X is wrong. Here's why
- The Shocking Truth about X
- The Great X Hoax
- 15 Things Your Favourite X Will Never Tell You
- What X Isn't Telling You about Y

These headline writers are using the power of a white lie to grab the attention of their readers. They are suggesting some deception because they know this will arouse curiosity within their readers. They know their readers will want to find out the truth.

Have a Little Something on the Side

If you're bored with your current writing project, cheat. Walk out on what you're doing, and start writing something that fires you up.

Having a writing project on the side can keep you motivated when your book, story or article is losing its lustre. This side-project will give you a new chance to turn up in front of the blank page when you want to do anything but.

Many successful writers cheat. They use pseudonyms for their creative side projects.

Stephen King wrote several horror novels under the pen name Richard Bachman as he wanted to publish more than one novel per year. Between 1977 and 2007, King published seven novels using this pen name including *The Running Man* and *Thinner*. King said he took on this side-project because he didn't want to oversaturate his brand. He's not the only high-profile author to take on a side-project or use a pen name.

In 2005, the Irish literary author John Banville won the prestigious Man Booker prize for his novel *The Sea*. Then in 2006, Banville published the first of his popular series of crime novels under the pen name Benjamin Black.

Several years ago, I attended a talk by John in Kerry where he explained why he sometimes use a pen name. He told a room of over 100 people he wanted to write something that wasn't so serious and that he could write and publish faster. He wanted a side-project he could turn to when he needed a break from writing literary fiction.

J.K. Rowling is another example of a writer with a side-project. She has published three crime fiction novels under the pen name Robert Galbraith.

"I had hoped to keep this secret a little longer, because being Robert Galbraith has been such a liberating experience. It has been wonderful to publish without hype or expectation, and pure pleasure to get feedback under a different name," said Rowling about her pseudonym.

Having a side-project gives writers opportunities to explore new writing styles and conventions that they typically wouldn't face in their day job. This form of deliberate writing practice will help you become a better writer. It will help you avoid the exhaustion and burnout that comes with focusing solely on a single niche or topic.

How Productive Writers Take On Side-Projects

If your day job involves writing reports, articles or copy for a website, you could write fiction in your free time. If spend most of your time writing blog posts, consider expanding one of these posts into a book or even a personal essay. And if you've just written a novel, try your hand at a short story in a different genre.

Before you cheat, remembers it's more important to finish one writing project than it is to attempt two at once. Now, if you're confident you have the time and motivation to write and finish two projects, have a little something on the side.

I won't tell anyone if you won't.

24

SEEK OUT QUIET SPACES

"Weakness of attitude becomes weakness of character."
– Albert Einstein

ARE YOU ABLE to work like Albert Einstein?

He was able to research and write some of his ground-breaking scientific papers while at home and surrounded by his two small children. Albert could write and think anywhere.

"Even the loudest baby-crying didn't seem to disturb Father," said Hans Albert about his father. "He could go on with his work completely impervious to noise."

Most of the rest of us don't have Albert Einstein's brains, talent or focus.

Carving out a quiet space in your house or workplace will help you write and think. Going to this place at the same time every day will make it easier for you to sit down in front of the blank page and write when you want to do anything but.

I have two small children, and I find it almost impossible to write when they are nearby. Instead, I get up early in the morning to write before they rise. I go to a small room near the front of the house and I write until they get up. This quiet time enables me to focus for longer and write more frequently than my failed attempts to write in the evenings when my house is noisier and busier.

Even if you don't have children, eliminate as many distractions as you can from your writing room or your office. This means no televisions, game consoles, mobile devices and, in certain cases, internet connections. A window, heating, and air conditioning are nice, but they're not necessary. A good desk, pens, paper and an idea are all you need.

In *On Writing* Stephen King says about having a quiet room in which to work, "Like your bedroom, your writing room should be private, a place where you go to dream. Your schedule — in at about the same time every day, out when your thousand words are on paper or disk — exists in order to habituate yourself, to make yourself ready to dream just as you make yourself ready to sleep by going to bed at roughly the same time each night and following the same ritual as you go."

Go Somewhere New to Write

I'm aware I'm contradicting myself, but a productive writer must be able to have two competing ideas in his or her head.

Hey, nobody said our craft is easy.

Writing in a new environment will break your mind free from the shackles of comfortable thinking. Going to a new location to write can get you out of a creative rut and help you overcome hurdles on the blank page. Sometimes, a new angle of attack will help you finish what you started.

At the end of the first *Star Wars* movie, Luke Skywalker flies into the trench of the Death Star. At first, Luke follows the same approach as every other fighter pilot and for a few terrible moments it looks like he will be killed by Darth Vadar's minions. Then, Obi-Wan Kenobi tells Luke to "use the Force". So, Luke turns off all his instruments and attacks the Death Star. Using this new approach, Luke succeeds at something no pilot had done before: he destroys the Death Star.

I use the *Star Wars* example because it's storytelling at its finest, and it shows that taking a different angle of attack can help you overcome a problem. In case you're not a Star Wars fan, I've dug up some scientific proof that supports writing in a new environment and coming at your project from an oblique angle.

A 2012 study in the *Journal of Consumer Research* found ambient or background noise positively affects creativity and increases the chances of innovative thinking.

"Results from five experiments demonstrate that a moderate (70 dB) versus low (50 dB) level of ambient noise enhances performance on creative tasks and increases the buying likelihood of innovative products," Mehta, Zhu and Cheema wrote.

The key takeaway from this report is to find somewhere with a comfortable but not distracting level of background noise. So, while a coffee shop may be appropriate, a playground full of children or a noisy bar won't help.

Managing Your Writing Environment

If you work in an office, you could write at another desk or even outside the office. I once worked in an office that had small rooms or booths that could only fit one person at a time. These booths were designed for making private phones calls away from the noise of the office, but I used these booths to write website copy and blog posts for this company. I found that I could get more done because I was less likely to be interrupted by the phone, email or even a colleague. Later, when I needed feedback about my copy, I went back to my desk and asked my colleagues for advice.

If your computer is the problem, leave it behind, take a notepad and a pen and go outside. The stimulation of a new environment combined with the openness of pen and paper may help you find your next sentence. There's something freeing about pen and paper and the lack of screen that opens the mind up to new ideas.

Alternatively, you could go to your local library and combine a morning's writing with an afternoon's research.

Several years ago I had to write a 40,000-word thesis. I found it easier to write my thesis in the college library even though I had a perfectly good office at home. This wasn't just because the library had everything I needed for my research; after all, I could have always rented the books I needed and took them home with me. There was something liberating about getting away from where I normally worked that made it easier to finish what I had started.

Sometimes, writers need a quiet place and a routine to get more done and sometimes they need to attack their project from a new angle. Or you could just use the Force.

Whatever works.

25

WRITE IN SHORT BURSTS

"I had to make sure I kept an eye on the real world."
– Roddy Doyle

SHORT WRITING SESSIONS are the best kind.

If you're struggling to develop a productive and regular writing habit, try writing every day for 15 or 30 minutes.

This is easier to achieve than sitting down in front of the blank page for several hours every other Sunday. It's also an achievable goal as almost every aspiring writer has 15-30 minutes in their day of which they can make better use.

If writing isn't your full-time job, short writing sessions are perfect for busy days. You could write between meetings, on the bus or train, before you leave for work or late in the evening. If you want to write in the evenings, you could skip a television programme, avoid the news or reduce the amount of time you spend on social media.

To get more from your next short writing session try

- Creating a list of topics to include in your article.

- Jotting down key words and ideas instead of full sentences

- Forgetting about perfect grammar, spelling or formatting

- Using pen and paper instead of a computer

- Setting yourself a challenge to produce as many words as possible within five, ten, twenty or thirty minutes

- Focusing on a single angle, section or paragraph
- Writing with the intention that you will fix or flesh out your ideas tomorrow

Short bursts of writing are like small wins. They accumulate over time until one day you look at your work and realise you've written ten thousand words.

How Roddy Doyle Wrote His Hit Novels In Short Bursts

The Irish author Roddy Doyle is famous for writing succinct and punchy sentences.

I attended a workshop about writing that he facilitated several years ago in Dublin.

There, Roddy explained that he wrote his earlier books during pockets of free time in the evenings. He also said that the sentences in earlier books like *The Commitments* and *The Snapper* are short because he wrote them while raising small children.

Roddy just didn't have time for lengthy, three-hour writing sessions, and if he didn't write in short bursts he wouldn't have written at all.

Doyle has even criticised other, more wordy books for being too long and unapproachable.

"*Ulysses* could have done with a good editor. You know people are always putting *Ulysses* in the top 10 books ever written but I doubt that any of those people were really moved by it," he famously said in New York in 2004.

I have two small children, and I can empathise with writers who must work within short blocks of time. Sometimes, the prospect of several hours work feels more intimidating than the job of sitting down for just thirty minutes to write. I also like short writing sessions because they make me feel like I've accomplished something for the day, and that can be enough to build the momentum needed to continue a troublesome writing project.

T.S. Eliot is another noted writer who wrote around the demands of his day. He worked at Lloyds Bank in London for much of his adult life, and he wrote book reviews and poetry in his free time. Eliot kept up his job in the bank even after he became an accomplished poet as his job provided him with a stabilising routine that he valued as a writer.

More recently, Roddy Doyle is quoted as saying that he now spends up to nine hours a day writing. Still, his experience and the experience of T.S. Eliot shows that a writer can finish what they started, even if they have personal commitments.

All you need is determination.

Conquer Procrastination and Develop a Daily Writing Practice

This time things were supposed to different.

Late last night, you promised yourself you'd write today. Then, you woke half an hour late for work. You got stuck in traffic and spent the day dealing with an angry customer/client/boss.

Later that evening at home, your kids needed help with their homework, and there were chores to do around the house.

When things were finally quiet, you didn't have the desire or the energy to sit down and do your most important work. Or maybe you forgot about your promise altogether.

To write every day is a simple ambition, and it's one many new writers struggle to achieve.

If you're having trouble, please don't give up.

I don't doubt your commitment or your talent; the only reason you don't write every day is because you haven't cultivated a daily writing practice.

In his book *The Power of Habit,* the author and journalist Charles Duhigg provides a simple but effective framework for creating habits. He says that

"Habits are a three-step loop— the cue, the routine, and the reward."

Set Up Your Cues for Writing

A habitual cue is something you see or do before you start writing. If you want to develop a writing practice, consider these cues.

Location: know in advance where you're going to write. This could be your office, a quiet room in your house or even a coffee shop.

Time: make a commitment to write at the same time every morning or evening. Don't make any plans that break this commitment

Emotional state: if you're stressed after a difficult day in the office, it's going to be harder to write. Figure out when you're calm and use this time for your best work.

Other people: writing is mostly a solitary activity, but the support of other writers is useful too. You could join a local writing group to hold yourself to account.

Immediately preceding action: whatever you do before you write should encourage your writing practice. If you're exhausted from spending the night at a party, you're not going to have much luck filling a blank page.

If you want to write every day, kill the cues for other habits that have nothing to do with your writing practice. Disconnect from the internet, remove the television from your workspace. Uninstall games from your computer. Do WHATEVER IT TAKES to keep your promise to protect your writing time and complete your most important work.

Establish Your Routine for Writing

Routines are powerful because we don't have to think about them. If you spend your day wondering how and where you're going to write, these questions will drain your mental willpower and make you more likely to say "I'll do it tomorrow." A good writing routine will help you overcome procrastination, become more productive and even shape your creative life.

If you want to spend less time thinking about your routine:

Gather what you need in advance: if you spend precious writing time searching for a laptop charger, your notes or for a file on your computer, you're already behind.

Use the same tools each time: I use Scrivener for almost all of my writing projects; whatever you use, the tool should never get in the way your writing.

Make a choice to trigger your cue: if you want to write in the morning, set your alarm clock for an hour earlier. If you want to write at night, turn off your phone and television and disconnect from the grid.

When you're starting out, it helps to decide in advance what you're going to write about.

Are you writing a blog post, short story or a chapter for your novel? What topic are you going to address today?

This decision will help you avoid the horrible moment when you sit down in front of the blank page and wonder "What now?"

Pick Your Reward for Writing

Writing is tough and even more so when you're starting out.

Go easier on yourself.

If you succeed in writing for twenty minutes, reward yourself with a treat like a cookie.

If you can chain three or four twenty minutes sessions together, go for a walk, a sleep or watch favourite TV programme guilt-free. And if you succeed in finishing an important writing project, buy something for yourself.

When I completed a 20,000-word research project, I bought an expensive a entertainment system that I otherwise couldn't have justified.

This reward system will trick your brain into associating pleasant activities with your writing practice.

Obviously it's not practical to eat a cookie (or to spend several hundred dollars) for every page.

However, as you become more confident you can extend the length and quality of your writing practice sessions and gradually remove these rewards.

If you succeed in cultivating a habit of writing every day, filling the blank page with your words and making small but determined progress towards a personal or professional goal will become a reward in itself.

Make a Plan and Stick To It

Once you've figured out your cue, routine, and reward for writing, have a plan for putting this into action. Duhigg suggests people can make a plan for habit change by keeping a diary.

Here's an entry in my writing diary:

Where am I? *At home*
What time is it? *07.00*
What's your emotional state? *Tired but calm*
Who else is around? *Wife and two children (asleep)*
What action preceded the urge to write? *My alarm clock went off*

I also sometimes record what I wrote about during writing practice and what I'd like to focus on next. I don't write entries like this all the time, but they help me when I'm stuck.

Seeking out this type of self-knowledge will help you identify your cue, routine and reward for writing.

Now You're Ready To Write Every Day

Creating a habit of daily writing practice isn't as difficult as it first seems. It takes determination and self-knowledge, and these are all traits every writer should cultivate.

Commit to this craft, and you will naturally become more determined as you progress. Learn to enjoy seeing your work improve, and you will come to value writing practice.

Take Duhigg's tips for cultivating a habit and you will gain the self-knowledge you need to write every day.

If you're about to apply this plan, I envy you.

One day, you'll stop typing, realise you've written 3,000 words in one session, and you'll wonder 'How the hell did I get here?'

Now, go write something.

26

TRACK YOUR PROGRESS

"Most people have dozens of things that they need to do to make progress on many fronts, but they don't yet know what they are." – David Allen

How MANY WORDS did you write today? Did you accomplish more than yesterday? And while I'm asking questions, did you write more this week or last week?

Almost every personal productivity strategy involves tracking your progress on some level because what gets tracked gets managed and what gets managed gets done.

Let me explain:

Professional athletes track themselves or use self-quantification techniques to record their diet, how much they lifted, how far they ran, and how many lengths they swam and so on. They use this information to train harder and smarter and to perform better in events. There's no reason why writers can't use this approach or self-knowledge to become more productive.

If you want to do this, you can track your time (which I'll cover in the next chapter) or you can track your output.

Know Thyself, Know Thy Word Count

Writers talk in terms of words counts rather than pages. They care less about page counts because the number of pages a piece takes depends on how the fonts, spacing and even the images are set and laid out. A page count is fluid, whereas a word-count is less so.

I've met writers who use daily word counts for personal competitions; they make a point of breaking their personal bests just like the runner in search of a faster time. I respect word counts because they can break a writer out of a creative funk and help you find something worthwhile to say. Knowing your average daily word count can also help you increase it.

For example, if your word count rises when you write in the morning and drops when you write at night, you can use this new information to cultivate an early morning writing habit.

According to the Paris Review, Ernest Hemingway recorded his daily word count on a large chart kept beneath a mounted gazelle head near where he wrote. He did this "so as not to kid myself".

There's just one caveat to obsessing about word counts.

They are no indication of quality, as a particular type of writing demonstrates.

Flash Fiction

Flash fiction is a special form of fiction writing for those who want to tell a story using as few words as possible. One of the most famous flash fiction stories (which may have been written by Hemingway) is just six words long. It reads:

"For sale: baby shoes, never worn."

Behold the power of brevity.

This why I also track how long I spend writing each week (more of that in the next chapter).

While working on this book, I set myself the goal of writing 10,000 words a week or 10 hours a week. I didn't mount a board under a gazelle head like Hemingway, instead I used a spreadsheet. Each Friday, I totalled up how long I spent writing and how many words I produced. This way, I could see how my book was progressing in terms of a word-count and hours spent writing.

This self-quantification helped me during the editing process too because although, I cared less about reaching a specific word-count, I still needed a goal to write towards.

Small Daily Wins

Getting the most from small daily wins means working on something a little every day and accomplishing it over time rather than trying to finish everything at the last minute. It's the productive person's equivalent of putting a euro or a dollar in a jar every day to save; it'll take you some time, but you'll get there in the end. If you want to harness the power of small daily wins, I recommend a simple trick invented by a famous (and rich) comedian.

Don't Break the Chain

The comedian Jerry Seinfeld invented this popular productivity trick to motivate himself to write one new joke every day. It's built on the principle of increasing your creative output through small, daily wins. I've used *Don't Break the Chain* to write feature articles, news stories, a thesis, various academic papers, blog posts and even this book.

If you procrastinate about sitting down in the front of the blank page regularly, this technique can help you get your ass into the chair. Here's how you do it:

1. Get a large calendar and pin it on the wall next to where you write

2. Write for 5, 10, 20 or 30 minutes

3. Using a felt pen, mark an X on your wall calendar through today's date

4. As the week progresses, write each day and build up a series or a chain of Xs

5. Now you have one job: *Don't Break the Chain*

Don't Break the Chain makes you feel guilty about ruining a productive writing streak. After all, nobody wants to a see a row of Xs for every day that you worked, only for this row to be broken in two because you stopped writing. I'm speaking from personal experience when I say, it's encouraging and reassuring to see the black Xs line up one after the other as a project processes. Each little X feels like a small victory in the war against procrastination.

This strategy is useful at the beginning of larger, more difficult writing projects. It gets you into the habit of turning up each day and slowly progressing your project. It will help you accept that, even if today's writing session doesn't go well, there is always tomorrow's session and the one after that. What's more important is that you turn up and put the work in.

There's just one problem with Seinfeld's technique. It's an unforgiving one because it makes no allowances for going on holidays, falling sick or for other personal commitments.

Hey, maybe Seinfeld doesn't get sick or take holidays?

Self-Knowledge Is Power

The productive writer knows how much she can accomplish on the blank page each day.

She uses the power of small daily wins to write consistently rather than leaving everything till the last minute. She knows it's better to turn up and do the work than it is to do nothing altogether.

27

MANAGE YOUR TIME

"It's really clear that the most precious resource we all have is time." – Steve Jobs

Do you know how to manage your time?

The productive writer does. He understands how long his writing projects will take, he takes charge of his other commitments so they don't impact on his work, and he gets the most out of the time he has for writing each day.

This is something I learnt the hard way.

For several years, I worked as a technology freelance journalist, and I made money through various writing commissions for magazines in Ireland. Although some commissions paid by the hour, I was still expected to complete them within a set period. For others, I was only paid for getting the job done.

This type of freelance work meant I earned less for my time if I spent twenty hours on a commission that should have only taken ten hours. I learned the hard way that making a living means finishing freelance projects on time.

Using the Calendar

Some professional writers block book periods for writing each morning and/or evening in their calendars. They avoid making personal or professional commitments during these times because they consider themselves 'committed' to their writing. They treat their craft like a job with professional obligations that must be honoured.

The calendar is the productive freelancer's best friend. It should be yours too. Get deadlines and appointments out of your head and into Google calendar, Outlook or some other tool you trust. Then, make a point to check your calendar each morning or evening.

At the end of every working week, you should also spend twenty minutes reviewing all the entries in your calendar. During this review, check what's coming up for the next seven days and how you spent your time over the previous seven days. While reviewing your calendar, ask questions like:

- What took up the most of my time last week?
- Are these activities likely to reoccur?
- What resources do I need to complete these activities faster?
- What do I need to prioritise next week?
- Am I likely to meet or miss my imminent deadlines?
- What's my most important task next week?

Editorial Calendars

Editorial calendars are another great way of managing your time, particularly if you work with other writers or if you are a blogger. The editors of professional media organisations use editorial calendars to plan writing projects in advance and to allow teams to juggle various projects.

You can use an editorial calendar to map your articles, stories, blog posts or chapters that you'd like to write over the next few months. They will help you gauge if you're progressing towards your writing goals. You can keep an editorial calendar in a notebook, a spreadsheet, a file on your computer or on a digital calendar. Whatever your tool of choice, an editorial calendar should identify some or all of the below:

- The topic
- The deadline

- The resources required
- The state of the project i.e. first draft, second draft etc.
- The publication date
- The priority of the writing project
- The media outlet or platform e.g. blog post, newsletter, social media

Making Friends With Deadlines

Deadlines are the productive writer's best friend; don't let anyone tell you otherwise.

Several years ago, I attended a workshop by the Irish short story writer, Claire Keegan. She explained that when she was starting off as a fiction writer, she used submission deadlines for short story competitions as something to work towards.

"Deadlines are not to be feared," she said. "They add a sense of urgency to our work."

Claire's point struck a chord with me, perhaps because I wasn't long out of college. Some writers (or students) leave writing projects till the last minute. When the deadline looms, they stay up late the night before smoking, drinking coffee and working hard on their current project. If you went to college, you're probably familiar with this last-minute approach.

Professional writers, like Claire, use deadlines to write more often. Amateur writers skip right past deadlines and tell editors their articles or stories will be ready when they're done.

If you're good, you can get away with telling your editor to wait. For the rest of us mere mortals, staying up late the night before a deadline may accomplish the task, but it's not a great way to work or write.

In the past, I missed deadlines because I was overworked, sick, unfocused and disorganised. My editors made allowances when I was overworked, understood when I sick, chastised me when I was unfocused and gave their next commission to someone else when I was disorganised.

If you're going to write for someone else, accept deadlines as part of your life. Respect them. Put them in your calendar and be honest about your ability to hit or miss them.

Deadlines give productive writers a goal or end-point to write towards. They force us to make decisions and *commit*. Yes, a looming deadline can cause stress and anxiety but this kind of tension is natural when it comes to hard work.

Tips for Meeting Your Deadlines

If you're having trouble meeting deadlines you could:

- Keep a list of your projects, assign a deadline to each project, and review this list each week
- Break projects into mini-projects with supporting deadlines
- Focus on the first or next action you need to take to advance a project
- Make more time for projects that are causing stress
- Diary your deadlines in a trusted system
- Communicate your deadlines to colleagues
- Negotiate or renegotiate deadlines
- Abandon projects that won't help you achieve your goals in favour of higher-value projects
- Question why you missed deadlines in the past
- Use existing deadlines as a reason for saying no to new projects

These days, I set myself artificial or soft deadlines for my writing projects. This helps me focus on what I'm writing, and it also gives me time to review and polish my work before publishing it. Even if this approach doesn't work for you, ask yourself why you missed deadlines in the past and how you're going to solve this problem.

As a productive professional writer, you must finish your writing projects on time. This is your job, and almost every writer will tell you that finishing one project before a deadline makes it easier to finish the next one, on time.

Getting Paid

Freelance journalists learn how to write fast. They need to eat, they need to sleep, and they need to get working on their next commission.

When I received my first 3,000-word commission from a national newspaper, I spent an entire week working on it. I carried out long, multiple interviews and spent hours researching the topic online and offline.

I probably shouldn't be telling you this, but much of my research and interviews were unnecessary. I had to cut this extra work from the piece, and I still struggled to finish the article on time. Later that month I was paid for the article itself and not how long I spent on it, which meant I'd put in a lot of unnecessary extra work.

I wasn't always paid per commission when I worked as a journalist. Several editors paid me in terms of hours spent on a writing project and not for how many words I wrote. These editors provided me with guidelines about how long a commission should take. In other words, I couldn't bill an editor for twenty hours work for a 300-word article.

Getting paid by the hour meant I had to complete writing projects within a set time period. If I spent too long on a commission, I was effectively paid less per hour. If I completed a project too quickly, it was either of poor quality (in which case my editor was quick to let me know) or I was paid less money.

So, I started tracking how long I spent on each commission using a timer on my computer and a spreadsheet. This information made it easier for me to invoice clients. This documentation also helped me figure out which types of commissions were easy to complete, which ones were more difficult, and how I could become a more productive writer. I also used this information to set prices for other clients and to decide on which commissions to accept and reject.

Figuring out how long to spend on a commission is a difficult balancing act. Give yourself some breathing room before you tell your editor how long you need. If you think a commission will take you six hours to complete, tell your editor it will take seven or eight hours.

This way, if there's an unforeseen circumstance (e.g. an interviewee cancelling at last minute), you will have extra time to complete your project. And if the commission only takes six hours, you can please your editor by under-promising and over-delivering.

Tracking your writing may seem tedious at first, but it will help you figure out which projects are taking longer than others, how you can complete these projects quicker and even if you should accept or reject certain projects in the future. This process will also save you time when it comes to submitting your invoices at the end of the month, and give you the confidence to negotiate a better rate from an editor or client.

Spending Your Reward

If you're having trouble managing how you spend your time on projects, review your calendar and commitments, do your most important work when you're productive, and track what's working and what's causing you problems.

Succeed and you will become a productive writer who has time to find new commissions or even to take a break. Fail to manage your time effectively and your work will either spill into your personal life or dry up.

Remember, the productive writer who manages her time effectively also gives herself permission to take a break. The productive writer knows when she needs to eat, sleep and recharge.

Most important of all, she knows when to stop.

28

FOCUS ON YOUR WORK

"It does not matter how slowly you go as long as you do not stop." – Confucius

FLOW IS A productive mental state whereby you are entirely focused on the task at hand. If you've ever exercised intensively or lost yourself to a piece of music, you've experienced flow. If you've ever started writing and lost track of the passage of time, you've experienced flow. It's a mental state you must seek if you want to become a more productive and accomplished writer.

An ability to focus on the task at hand is a great skill to cultivate. The problem is technology wants us to do anything but. Phones, emails, notifications, feeds, applications, and updates all pull on our attention throughout the day.

According to a report by Carnegie Mellon University, published in the *New York Times*, a typical officer worker is interrupted every 11 minutes. The researchers found it can take 21 minutes to refocus on a task, once interrupted. This finding suggests it's almost impossible for the average office worker to experience flow because of these day-to-day interruptions.

Writing is not meant to be multi-tasked with answering email, checking social media and attending to the 1,001 other demands of day-to-day life. It's just too damn hard. If you approach your craft with a start-stop-start mind-set, you will never achieve the kind of flow writers need to reach the end of whatever it is you are working on.

The productive nature of multi-tasking is another pernicious myth that productive writers must expose. It taxes your brain, and it makes it even harder to finish what you're working on.

MIT neuroscientist Earl Miller told NPR in 2008, "Switching from task to task, you think that you're actually paying attention to everything around you at the same time. But, you're not."

A true writer can't pay attention to everything around them at the same time.

How can you write one true sentence when you're checking your friend's holiday photos on Facebook?

How can you craft a perfect call-to-action for your copy when you're on the phone with a colleague?

How can you massage a paragraph into something readable when you're clicking from one blog post or website to another searching for something, *anything* that backs up your argument?

Commit yourself entirely to writing, and then when you're finished writing for the day, commit yourself entirely to whatever else is important.

How To Maintain Focus and Flow

Did you ever sit down to write and almost immediately think of something you forgot to look up?

When was the last time you put down your writing so you could research a new angle for your work?

Do you sometimes put down your pen and pick up a book to check a fact or a quote?

Research forms the backbone of many successful writing projects.

Academic writers, journalists, bloggers and writers interview experts, read books, search for topics online and go through the archives of their libraries. Many writers enjoy research because they get to spend time talking to people and learning about topics in their area of interest. They enjoy it because writers like reading and finding out new things.

Research is an altogether different skill to writing, however. It involves moving from one question to the next, following a thread or searching for a specific piece of information. Writing, on the other hand, means working deliberately on one sentence or idea for an extended period without giving up. These two activities are almost impossible to undertake simultaneously. You can't jump from one topic to the next and concentrate entirely on a sentence or an idea.

The next time you're writing, and you want to check an important fact or even how a word is spelt, whatever you do, *don't stop writing*.

If you do, you will break your flow of concentration and possibly disappear down a rabbit hole of meaningless Google searches and needless research.

Instead, **annotate** the section of the document you are writing with an asterisk, an X or with your writing programme's annotation tool. When you've hit your target word count for the day, address these annotations. Commit yourself entirely to writing and entirely to research, just not at the same time. When I work this way, I'm always amazed by how a seemingly important question didn't need to be answered after all.

Similarly, **keeping a notepad and pen at your desk** will help you concentrate on what you're writing.

Use this notepad to record and ideas or thoughts that come to mind. Record things you want to look up on the internet, people you want to call and food you have to buy. If a colleague drops by your desk with a request, record their request and then keep writing.

Unless the task or request is urgent, like a hungry child or an iron still plugged in, don't get up and do it. Later, when you're finished writing, you can spend time attending to the tasks on your notepad.

The purpose of annotating your work and using a notepad is to help you maintain a sense of flow.

This way, you can concentrate on your work and later, you can concentrate on whatever else you want to do.

How The Productive Writer Keeps Going

The productive writer knows it's difficult to get into the mindset needed to finish a project. He knows multitasking is a dangerous myth that stands in the way of his word count.

He knows his research and writing are two different activities. He knows this because this is how he finishes what he started.

29

LET YOUR WRITING FERMENT

"The truth will set you free. But not until it is finished with you."
– David Foster Wallace

Do you enjoy the taste of wine?

The best tasting vintages are left to ferment for weeks, months, or even years in a cool, dark place before being decanted into bottles.

Winemakers and drinkers know the product becomes better with age. Writing is a little like making fine wine.

There's the gathering of the ingredients, equipment, and materials. There's the artistry, hard-work, craft, and inevitable wait for something good.

When you've worked on a difficult writing project at length, it's hard to know what to remove and what to keep.

When you're writing with flavour, should you cut a chapter or expand a key point? Should you insert more research or write a personal story?

These creative problems can become so exhausting you just want your writing project to end.

These types of creative problems are also natural. The more you write, the easier it'll become to accept this.

Your Cool Dark Place

Don't publish a piece of writing immediately after it's done.

It'll be too raw and bitter for public consumption. Every writer needs a dark place for their work to ferment.

Leave your early drafts in a drawer and take this time to rest, to write something else, and to forget about what's fermenting in your drawer. Later, you can take this writing out into daylight and taste it. You can approach it with an editing pen and a set of fresh eyes.

Thanks to this time away from your work, you will discover flaws and gaps you overlooked. You'll be able to address your problems with a renewed vigour. You'll be able to write with flavour.

Unlike before, this rewrite will feel more natural. The solutions you searched for last time round will be within your reach.

When you finally publish your writing, your readers will enjoy the taste more, because you gave the flavour time to develop.

How Long Should You Let Your Writing Ferment?

The time a piece of writing belongs in a drawer depends on how long it is, who it's for, and your other professional commitments .

Here's what I do:

I let blog posts rest a day or two before publishing them. This is because it's easy and fast to edit or change a blog post. If it's a longer article, I wait a week or more before sending it to an editor.

This is because I've professional relationships with editors, who expect a certain standard of work.

I've also put my short stories and book chapters in a drawer for several months, until I've almost forgotten what they're about.

This gives me time to cast a fresh eye over my work, remove clichés (there's one), ttypos (there's another), and fix other structural problems.

These different fermentation periods give me the distance I need to improve my writing.

I embrace this time away, because when I finally take my writing from the drawer, I'm fresh enough to expand, clarify, or condense my points and sentences.

I have the energy to back up my arguments with some additional or much-needed research.

Thanks to the drawer, I can face that much needed, and often dreaded, rewrite with a thirst to fix what's broken. The drawer is a good place to let your writing ferment, but as a professional writer, you won't always be able to rely on this luxury.

What Professional Writers Do

Professional writers can't always put a piece of writing into a drawer and let it sit for weeks at a time. This is because they have to work to deadlines imposed by editors, contracts, publications, and even their readers. This is why professional writers don't work alone.

They invariably have the support of editors, who can (hopefully) catch these errors and mistakes and help them fix them. If the editor is supportive, they will show the writer how to avoid making these types of errors again. Becoming a professional writer means enlisting an editor, who serves as your ally in the war against perfectionism.

Behold the Myth of Perfectionism

Writing with flavour doesn't mean waiting for the day when it's finally perfect. Even wine becomes undrinkable if it's left to ferment too long.

Remember: The perfect creative work doesn't exist.

There will always be a vast chasm between your ideas and how your words gather on the page. This chasm makes many writers and creative people feel squeamish.

It was the philosopher, Nietzsche, who said, "And if thou gaze long into an abyss, the abyss will also gaze into thee."

When I see my words arranged on the page, I remember everything has already been said and in more ways than I can ever imagine.

The gaze of all those more talented and creative writers from times past gazes back at me. And I want to jump.

So I turn away.

And I press publish.

What Happens When You Say Not Today?

If you insist on endlessly polishing and rewriting your work, you will delay your writing projects indefinitely.

This procrastination will frustrate colleagues, clients, and readers (yes, your readers!), who are waiting on you to finish your work.

Perfectionism is a dangerous myth for which productive writers should be watchful.

I hate to break it to you, but perfectionism is an excuse for putting off publishing your work. These types of excuses are indulgent.

Eventually, they turn the productive writer into a miserable and procrastinating one.

The good news is, you can overcome perfectionism today.

Overcoming Perfectionism and Procrastination

In a 1996 interview with WYNC, the American essayist and author David Foster Wallace explained the dangers of perfectionism:

"You know, the whole thing about perfectionism. The perfectionism is very dangerous, because of course if your fidelity to perfectionism is too high, you never do anything.

"Because doing anything results in– It's actually kind of tragic because it means you sacrifice how gorgeous and perfect it is in your head for what it really is."

I try to remember Wallace's advice when I approach the end of a writing project. I also set publication dates for my writing and do my best to stick to them. I also try not to take the writing so seriously.

All I can do is keep practicing, keep falling forwards, and keep using these painful writing lessons to improve my work.

If you're struggling to expose the myth of perfectionism in your writing, don't endlessly work and rework your writing alone.

It's more effective to ask someone you trust to critically evaluate your writing and offer feedback than it is to work alone.

So, who can you ask for help?

This could be an editor, a trusted friend, a member of your writing group, or an honest family member.

The only caveat is this person must be able to offer you candid feedback you will act on.

Don't wait years to publish your writing.

Accept doubt as part of the process and understand you must share your writing with the world. Put it in the drawer and let your writing develop. Then take it out and expose your writing to the world.

Let them love it or hate it and all its ugly imperfections.

30

ASK FOR HELP

"We are all here on earth to help others; what on earth the others are here for I don't know." – W.H. Auden

THERE'S NO SHAME in it.

Writing may be a solitary craft, but if you're going to write anything significant or accomplish more you need help, and it comes in many forms.

You could look for a more experienced writer to act as your mentor or you join a local writing group. You may need to hire a designer to create a cover for your ebook or images for your website. Or you could hire someone to market and publicise your work or your business.

Yes, you can learn how to do all of these things yourself, but consider where your time is better spent: learning a skill secondary to your craft or writing?

Don't be all things when one is enough. The secret to becoming a more productive writer is to leverage your strengths and offset your weaknesses.

- Can you find an assistant for your research?
- Can an editor help you organise your work?
- Should you a hire a designer to create your book cover so you can concentrate on writing?
- Do you need a developer to manage the technical parts of your website?

I paid a designer to create a cover for this book. I could have done this myself, but the results wouldn't have been as professional, and my time is better spent writing. Similarly, I know a successful blogger who writes outlines for his posts. He gives these outlines to an editor to complete and format in WordPress. The blogger says writing like this enables him to finish up to eight blog posts per week.

The longer you work on a piece, the harder it is to see your mistakes and figure out if you have gone astray. What's interesting to you may not be interesting to the reader.

If you haven't talked to any readers, then how can you know?

Friends and family, if they will be honest with you, are a good start. They can help your proofread your work and offer advice on how to improve. Or you could ask colleagues to check if your copy is getting the job done.

If your friends or colleagues are any good, they'll come back with suggestions for words and ideas you can remove, include or rework. They'll probably pick up a few typos that you missed too.

Don't let your writing in all its ugliness expose itself to the world. Get help now before it's too late.

Fall In Love with Feedback

If you write, you must seek out feedback.

I was a member of a creative writing and non-fiction writing group in Dublin for several years.

They hated almost everything I wrote.

These more accomplished writers told me how I could improve my work.

So I listened.

Other more accomplished writers expose you to new kinds of writing and new ways of looking at your work. They encourage and push you to write beyond anything you've attempted before.

You could join a writing group in your local community or join a writing group online. If you write non-fiction, there are a number of professional online writing courses and communities you can join.

Not every writer needs to join a writing group, however.

I interviewed the famous Irish novelist Jennifer Johnston several years ago. Since 1972, she has published over 20 books and numerous plays. Jennifer told me she has little time for creative writing groups.

"They take you away from your work," she said. "I didn't need them."

Jennifer didn't need a writing group, but she is an exception. Her father Denis was a famous playwright, and he provided Jennifer with the feedback Jennifer needed to improve.

Unless you're Jennifer or you've someone like Denis who can review your work, joining a writing group is beneficial. It encourages accountability, and it opens you up to criticism. You also get to spend time in the company of other writers and learn from their experiences.

Not everything these people have to say will be correct or of value, just like not everything you write will succeed or have merit.

Finding this out is half the fun.

Find Your Mentor

Do you have a mentor for your writing?

Finding a mentor who knows more about writing than you do is a short-cut to better prose. I've met several people who helped me improve my writing.

A tutor in university explained how to write for an academic audience. An instructor in a creative writing class showed the students and I how to improve our prose and kill our darlings. An English teacher in school taught me how to bend any topic towards an idea that I wanted to write about. And an editor I didn't get along with demonstrated how to write clearly and without obvious bias.

Some of these people knew they were mentoring me; some of them didn't.

I never even met one of my mentors. His name is John Cheever, and he died in 1982, one year after I was born.

So, how can John Cheever be my mentor?

Several years ago, I considered abandoning writing altogether. My freelance contracts had dried up, I'd received multiple rejection letters from various competitions and editors, and my writing was rotting in my drawer.

Then, I discovered *The Journals of John Cheever*. I'd read some of Cheever's short stories before, but his journals are a different beast entirely. In it, he wrote about his personal demons and his journey towards becoming an accomplished writer. Through reading his works, I rediscovered my passion for writing, and I found a reason to keep going..

Even today, when I become disillusioned with the act of writing, I think of Cheever's mantra that a "good page of prose remains invincible". I think of him writing day after day through a difficult marriage, alcoholism, depression, being a parent, happiness and success.

No matter what, John wrote.

Save Time by Modelling Your Creative Mentors

Another great way to get the most from your mentor or an expert you admire deeply is to apply as many of their practices as possible. This process is called **modelling**, and it will help you achieve mastery faster.

In his book *Mastery*, Robert Greene explains how this process works:

"The key then to attaining this higher level of intelligence is to make our years of study qualitatively rich. We don't simply absorb information - we internalise it and make it our own by finding some way to put this knowledge to practical use."

By modelling your creative betters, you can avoid many of the mistakes your mentors made on their way to success and save time because they will have done the hard work of sifting through good and bad information for you.

No, I'm not advocating you steal your mentor's work.

Instead, figure out a way to get close to your creative hero and learn from them ethically.

Today, many creators and writers offer online courses and coaching classes that you can sign up for where they will teach you what they know. If this isn't possible, read as much of their work as you can get your hands on. Whatever your approach, absorb and implement as many lessons as you can from your mentor(s). To avoid becoming overwhelmed, focus on learning only from one or two mentors at a time. Then, when you've learnt or applied as many of their lessons as you can, find your next mentor.

Handling Criticism Like a Pro

The first time I wrote an article for a newspaper my editor hated it. He told me he wasn't going to publish my work.

"If you don't improve your writing, I'm going to fire you," he said.

I went into the bathroom, sat on the toilet and thought about quitting. What kind of person was I? Was I lazy and incompetent? Did I deserve to be fired?

Up till this point, everybody had told me I could write. My identity was intimately connected with the idea of being a writer and if an accomplished writer like my editor hated my work, then who was I?

The first time I submitted a short story to a creative writing group, the instructor of the group announced to the class that my story reminded him of a hammy B-movie.

"You need to spend more time writing something we can believe in," he said.

I went home and tore up the short story I was working on. What was the point in wasting so much time working on a story only for another person to hate it?

Perhaps my nights were better spent watching television?

It took time, but I accepted their criticism. They were right. My article was terrible and my short stories were stuffed with clichés. I vowed to try harder. I promised myself I'd improve.

Now I seek criticism out. Praise is useful but negative feedback is more valuable. It gives the productive writer a chance to expose a fault in their craft and fix it.

Some criticism may be constructive, and some of it won't help at all. But your fiercest critics could become your biggest enablers for better writing.

My favourite story of a writer embracing criticism involves the social media guru and business author, Gary Vaynerchuk. One disappointed customer left a negative one star review of Gary's, *Crush It* book on Amazon.

Gary's reply?

"Frank. I am so so sorry I under delivered for you, I hope to meet u and spend 15 minutes apologizing and answering any questions u may have, I guess I needed more details in there for u, I am so sorry."

The next time you finish what you're working on, seek out criticism.

Ask your friends, your family and your enemies to tell you what they love and hate about your work. Use their feedback to become a better, stronger, more accomplished kind of writer.

31

LEARN TO EDIT

"If it sounds like writing, I rewrite it." – Elmore Leonard

EDITING IS THE process of reviewing, arranging, and polishing your work, so it makes sense for readers.

After you have finished the first draft, zoom out from your writing and consider it as a whole.

Assess if the introduction and the conclusion are appropriate and if one paragraph leads into the next. Consider whether your writing supports your central argument, thesis, or narrative all the way through.

Then, polish your prose and remove as many unnecessary words and sentences as possible.

Look at ways to break your work into more digestible chunks.

Could you make your work more readable by breaking it into chapters or sections or by using sub-headings, lists, and bullet-points?

There's nothing wrong with thousands of words of uninterrupted prose but, unless you're shit hot, it's far more difficult to keep your readers' attention with this type of writing.

Even lengthy feature articles are broken up with standout quotes, pictures, and subheadings.

If you're writing for the web, this styling is more important, because most of your readers won't stay on a webpage for over two minutes.

When you've completed your first draft, get a pen, print out your work, and strike out as many unnecessary words and sentences as possible.

Below, I've highlighted filler words and phrases you should look out for and explained why they are unnecessary:

"I'm **quite** sure."

You are? You sound unsure.

"I **really** don't know."

I know you talk like this, but do you need to write like this?

"I've got **stuff** to do."

That's vague, can you tell me what you have to do?

"I'm **literally** sick of this."

Are you sick, should I call a doctor?

"**Maybe** I should just go."

You sound unsure.

"Perhaps, you're too clever."

I am too clever; I'm sorry.

"An apology is **very** unnecessary."

How can an apology be unnecessary or very unnecessary?

"I'm glad **that** we understand each other."

I'm glad we understand each other.

"**In conclusion,** I promise to work harder."

You're going to work harder? I get it.

The highlighted words and phrases above are weak, and they prevent clear and effective communication between you and your reader.

Writers use them as stand-ins when they can't think of anything else or when they haven't polished their work. They belong in a first draft, but not in a second.

Eliminate adverbs from your writing too

Bad fiction is full of them. Adverbs are basically (there's one!) words that end in -ly.

Adverbs are often redundant. They hinder what you want to say, and they make sentences longer.

Consider:

"Give it to me!" she shouted **angrily**.

"Please don't make me," he pleaded **fearfully**. "It's mine."

Now, consider these stronger and more compelling revisions:

"Give it to me!" she shouted.

"Please don't make me," he pleaded. "I need it."

Again, the highlighted words and phrases above are weak and wordy. Use adverbs as little as possible in your writing or not at all.

If you need to find adverbs, open the last thing you wrote in your word processor of choice and search it for words that end with 'ly'.

Then, ask yourself if you can delete what comes up. The point of this brutal editing is to cut the chaff and refine your work.

Use the Active Voice

Do you use the active voice?

If you're a writer, you should.

It's the best way to invigorate whatever you're working on. The active voice demonstrates continued action on behalf of the subject. For example, "I threw my pen at the wall" contains an active verb.

In this case, "I" is the subject and "threw" is the active verb.

Here are three great examples of the active voice in action:

- "I wrote a blog post about grammar."
- "He read a novel in one night."
- "She ran a marathon in under four hours."

In each case, it's clear what the subject did. We don't need to read a sentence twice.

If you're a writer, the passive voice is your enemy.

The passive voice demonstrates how the subject of a sentence changes because of an action.

For example, "The pen was thrown at the wall" uses the passive voice. In this example, the state of the pen changes as a result of an action.

Now consider:

- "The blog post about grammar was written by me."
- "The novel was read by him in one night.
- "The marathon was run by her in under four hours."

These sentences are boring to read, because they rely on the passive voice.

Yes, sometimes, writers must use the passive voice, but these occasions are rare. You can use the passive voice when emphasising the subject of your sentence is important.

Consider: "The term 'penicillin' is often used generically to refer to…"

Here, the author is writing a scientific document about penicillin.

You can also use the passive voice if you are being deliberately vague.

Sometimes, journalists use the passive voice when the facts of a news story are unclear, and they want to avoid defamation.

Consider: "The car was stolen last night."

Here, we don't know who stole the car.

The passive voice is also common in scientific and technical documents, where the writer describes instructions or events.

"The penicillin was mixed with…"

These examples are boring to read. If you are writing a blog post, article, story, newsletter, or copy, use the active voice wherever possible.

It will grab your reader's attention in a way that boring, passive voice sentences never can.

Relying on the passive voice is a turn-off for your reader. Writers reach for the passive voice when they're tired, lazy, or unsure of what to say next.

Keep Your Cut-offs

Where do your unpublished blog posts and articles, leftover research, and abandoned chapters go?

To become a more productive writer, they belong in a digital or paper-based file you review and refer to often.

These abandoned ideas may not have made it into your current writing project, but there may be a future opportunity to turn your cut-offs into more rounded and usable ideas.

Relying on your cast-offs isn't a shortcut, and it's not cheating; let no one tell you otherwise.

If a carpenter can reuse wood for a new project and a technician can reuse computer parts, why can't a writer return to his or her abandoned ideas?

Writers shouldn't have to reinvent themselves every time they are presented with a new writing project.

If we did that, we wouldn't have time to finish anything.

Not everything you discard will be of merit, but why take the chance of letting a semi-formed idea disappear into the ether?

If you researched a topic, only to find you couldn't use what you found, you could always draw on this research for your next project.

Or, if you've argued a point only to edit it entirely, you can use parts of your argument in a future article, blog post, or chapter.

Keeping your cuttings is one way to overcome writer's block and advance troublesome projects because, instead of staring at a blank page, you can peruse your old musings.

Sometimes, I take an abandoned idea and use it as a jumping off point into something new.

I've written dozens of blog posts that were never published, and I've interviewed many people, only to set aside large portions of what they had to say.

In both cases, I've used extracts from my abandoned blog posts and interview transcripts for new writing projects.

Even if you never use your cut-offs, they don't represent wasted time or energy.

Instead, consider them as markers on the path towards a more polished and coherent work. For a productive writer, nothing is ever lost or wasted.

32

LIVE WITH FAILURE

"Productivity is being able to do things that you were never able to do before." – Franz Kafka

IF YOU WANT to become a more productive writer, accept you're going to fail time and again.

I've written dozens of blog posts and articles that nobody read. I've pitched article ideas to editors that were rejected. I've published articles only to find they contained typos or even factual errors. I've also spent hours preparing stories and articles for various competitions only to find they weren't even long-listed.

I was disappointed by each one of these failures and, at times, I even questioned what I was doing. However, my collection of failures gave me the opportunity to improve my writing and to learn something of myself. On the occasions that I passed these opportunities up, I met with the same failures weeks or months later.

Failing is part of living. Like the runner who falls down while training, a writer must get back up again after failing and keep on going. The only other option is stopping altogether, and that's not a realistic choice for anyone who is passionate about the written word.

You can write about your failures and how they've shaped who you are. You can explain how your failures helped you become the person you are today. You can also describe how you overcame some failures and learnt to live with others.

There are hundreds of writers who only became successful after their death.

For example, many critics cite *Moby Dick* as one of the greatest works of all time, but Herman Melville didn't live to see it receive acclaim.

Czech author, Franz Kafka broke new ground with *The Metamorphosis* and *The Trial*, but he wrote in obscurity in Austria and the Czech Republic during the late 19th and early 20th century. Before his death, Kafka asked his friend Max Brod to burn his letters (thankfully Brod ignored Kafka's request).

Emily Dickinson struggled for much of her life to find anyone that would print her work. She famously received this rejection letter from a publisher:

"Your poems are quite as remarkable for defects as for beauties and are generally devoid of true poetical qualities."

Forget What You've Achieved

Are you holding onto the past?

If you are, it could be holding you back from accomplishing more.

Before he died, John Cheever told the *Paris Review* he felt a "sense of clinical fatigue" after finishing a novel. Despite the success of his short stories, he described having little time for many of them after they were published.

"I love them, but I can't read them; in many cases, I wouldn't love them any longer if I did," he said in 1969.

Lots of writers and artists say they can't bear to look on their old work and once they're done with something, they never want to see it again. It took me some time to understand why.

As I progressed from one media organisation to the next, I built a portfolio of articles, news stories and clippings that I was proud of. I cut these clippings out and stored them carefully in an expensive leather case.

I told myself this portfolio was for potential employers. It was my insurance policy against future unemployment and I believed that every accomplished journalist kept these types of portfolios.

Witness my exercise in vanity.

By keeping this portfolio, I was holding onto past successes. I was telling myself I didn't need to move forward as a writer because "Look!

I've already been published and in a national newspaper. Surely I'm good enough."

I wasn't good enough. Many of my articles were badly written or poorly researched. Part of me knew this but in keeping my portfolio, I was holding onto past failures.

My clippings reminded me of missed opportunities. They reminded me of promising jobs that came to an abrupt end and of stories that felt important at the time but which meant nothing weeks or months later. I couldn't live like this. Something had to change.

One Saturday morning, I gathered old boxes, various broken appliances and some empty paint cans and my portfolio. I put them in the car, and I drove to the dump. There, I threw everything into the skips.

Keeping this portfolio was holding me back from seeing new opportunities, such as a college course I wanted to take and later a blog that I wanted to start.

After throwing my old clippings and articles away, I felt empty but, like any empty vessel, I was ready for something new. I was able to go home and consider how I was going to make a living from writing without trying to become a successful journalist. I was able to fall forwards.

I'm not advocating writers should disown their work once they're done with it. Instead, take some time to consider if your older articles (the ones you're proud of) are adding value to your craft today or if you're just holding onto the past.

For example, the blogger and author Johnny B. Truant, describes in his book *Write. Publish. Repeat.* how he was originally known as a motivational coach and a blogger. This was "Johnny 1.0", he writes. When he became more well-known writing science fiction and horror books like *The Beam* and *Fat Vampire*, he removed his old works from Amazon and reinvented himself.

"[My old books] fit me so poorly, in fact, that I actually asked Amazon to remove them from my author page so they wouldn't distract my fiction readers," he writes.

Remember, it's better to try and fail, to fall forwards and learn what you can from these experiences than it is to sit on the couch and do nothing.

33

FINISH WHAT YOU STARTED

"Whatever it takes to finish things, finish. You will learn more from a glorious failure than you ever will from something you never finished." – Neil Gaiman

WHEN WAS THE last time you took 30 minutes out from your week to review how your writing is going? Would you like to see how your writing is progressing? Is there a way of figuring out what you need to write next and what you should stop doing?

There's a simple strategy that can help you answer all of these questions and gain some control over your writing. It's called the weekly review.

I learnt about the weekly review several years ago from David Allen (the author of Getting Things Done). It's a strategy for business people and professionals to take charge of their lives, but it's a useful one for writers who want to accomplish more too. Since putting this strategy into practice, I've found it to be a great way of taking charge of my writing and even other areas of my life.

The weekly review gives me confidence that I'm writing the right things at the right time, and it helps me shine a light on neglected parts of my creative or writing life.

The good news is a weekly review doesn't take a lot of time or extra work to implement.

The Weekly Review for Writers

At the end of the week, put aside 30-60 minutes for your weekly review. If it's helpful, book this time in your calendar as a recurring appointment and make a commitment to keeping it.

Use this time to stop writing, zoom out and gain some perspective over your work. The goal of your weekly review is to figure out what you accomplished over the past few days, what you overlooked and what you need to do or write next. During your review, be honest with yourself. Ask and answer questions like:

- What did I accomplish or write this week?
- What went well/didn't go well?
- What are my most important task(s) for next week?
- What was my word-count for the week?
- How many hours did I spend writing?
- How many ideas did I generate?
- How did I market my writing or my work?
- What events are in my calendar for the previous/next seven days that I need to act on?
- What have I been putting off?
- What should I stop doing or say no to?

Remember, this review is not the time for working on your projects or for writing.

You should use your weekly review to clarify your priorities and make plans for future writing projects. This may mean adding missing activities or upcoming deadlines to your calendar or even deciding if you need to renegotiate commitments with your editor or clients. If you use a To Do list, this is the time to update it with new items and to remove old items that you have no intention of completing.

You can ask and answer these questions in a journal if you like. When you've answered these questions and you're clear about what you need to do next, you'll be able to hit the blank page feeling better about yourself and your work.

During the weekly review, I file my research, organise my notes and quickly read through the ideas I came up with during the week. This helps me evaluate if there's anything I've overlooked or if there's an idea I can use over the coming days in my work.

I also write down or mark minor accomplishments during the week such as hitting a target word count or completing a book chapter. These minor creative accomplishments are important to mark and a great way of keeping motivated. Think of it this way: paragraphs make up book chapters, and finished chapters will fill a book. In other words, the accumulation of these minor accomplishments contributes to a major one.

The weekly review is a powerful productive strategy, which if used correctly, will help you plan for future writing projects secure in the knowledge that you have the resources and time to finish what you started.

What Lies Ahead

Finishing what you started writing isn't so tough now that you know how to manage your time, and commitments. The good news is once you get into the habit of finishing, the rewards are immense. You'll get:

Your hands dirty: Studying the work habits and creative strategies of writers like Ernest Hemingway and John Caples is fun, but writing isn't a spectator sport. You'll learn more of this craft by wading in up to your neck.

To bleed: Great writers bleed onto the page and leave a part of themselves behind. This is living, and the following day, these writers do it all over again.

The opportunity to make mistakes: If you ship your work and it's badly received, you can use this feedback to become a better writer. If you don't ship, you won't get feedback, and you'll never get a chance to improve.

Smarter: Finishing a piece trains your brain to make new connections and come up with better ideas for your next writing project.

Answers to the questions that keep writers up at night: Are you a non-fiction writer, a copywriter, a story-teller or a genre fiction writer? Finishing your work will help you answer these questions because you'll know more of what you enjoy and what you're good at.

Over the blindspots in your practice: Do you have trouble writing strong introductions? What can you do to write better headlines? How can you deepen your research? Treasure the difficult moments; they are the foundations of your writing practice.

Faster!: You're an athlete and writing is a race. It may be a sprint, a ten-mile event or a marathon. Whatever the length of your work, get through it and you'll finish the next one faster.

The confidence that comes with finishing: When your article appears in print, your short story in a magazine or your blog post on a popular site, you'll feel lighter than you have in months. Then, when you sit down to write again, you'll be hungry for more success.

A free education: If you guest post for a popular website, you'll have the chance to talk to another editor who can help you improve your work and (if the relationship goes well) provide you with opportunities for future work. This is the kind of feedback people pay money for.

Paid: Professional writers turn up, they do the work and they move on. And they get paid. You deserve to get paid too.

BECOMING THE PRODUCTIVE WRITER

Writing will always feel like a messy and sometimes disjointed pursuit that doesn't fit neatly into any box or To Do List. That doesn't mean you can get away with missing deadlines and permanently unfinished projects. These are the hallmarks of amateurs who don't know where they're going or what they're doing. If you made it this far, you're not an amateur.

Several years ago, I was an amateur (albeit one who had convinced some people otherwise).

I worked as a journalist for a local newspaper in Ireland. It was my job to write news stories each week, to cover the council meetings, political speeches and business stories in the area. This job was my first real one since graduating from college, and I saw it as my big break into the big, bad, wide world of print journalism.

For a man with such ambitions for his career, I had one big problem.

I spent more time talking to people in the office, reading the news online and doing anything but my job. Eventually, my procrastination caught up with me.

One sunny Wednesday morning, after I'd missed a big deadline the night before, my editor called me into the office. He told me to close the door and take a seat. You know it's not good when they tell you to take a seat.

"I'm not happy with your progress here Bryan, you're letting things slip," he said leaning back in his chair. "The reality is if you can't finish the damn thing, you're not doing your job, and if you're not doing your job, this newspaper will have to let you go."

"I can do better, I can explain," I said. "Give me another chance."

I didn't deserve another chance and I had no genuine excuses. My editor was right. I wasn't doing my job. Luckily though, he didn't fire me (at least not that day).

Since then, I've made every possible mistake writing fiction and non-fiction. I've learnt the hard way that finishing something, anything, gives a writer the confidence to write again.

If you can't finish the damn thing, you're not doing your job. You're not fulfilling the challenge productive writers like Stephen King laid down for the rest of us.

Ask yourself:

- What's the last writing project you abandoned?
- When was the last time you published or submitted a writing project for publication?
- Are you constantly seeking new ways to get feedback about your writing?
- When will you finish what you're writing?
- Why are you procrastinating?

If you finish what you are working on, you will feel a sense of accomplishment alien to the writer who gave up altogether. Creating, writing and finishing your work will teach you far more than polishing pages of prose for months on end.

Whether you're writing fiction or non-fiction, shipping is more important than perfection. Instead of abandoning a writing project or slaving away indefinitely, set a target for submission or publication.

Stick to this target and, if you miss it, finish, publish or submit your work as soon as you can.

There's no need to ship mediocrity or publish a writing project for the sake of it; just don't let your writing stagnate in a drawer.

Confidence comes when you reach the end.

When you finish your next writing project, some people may criticise or reject your work. They could be right, but you still gain a victory.

Even if your writing project is a failure, at least you will be free to write something else, something better.

I've finished a lot of awful articles in my time, but finishing gave me the confidence to see the writing process through. Afterwards, I was able to show people my work (warts and all) and learn from their feedback. Feedback is invaluable. It's your chance to learn how to become a better writer for free.

If you get into the habit of finishing your work, you can become a writer who thinks of an idea, fleshes it out, edits, rewrites, polishes and then rewrites some more, before finishing the damn thing.

None of this is possible if you get hung up on creating the perfect piece of writing.

My editor and I long since fell out, but I'm still writing.

Are you?

WHAT ARE YOU WAITING FOR?

PLEASE KNOW THAT words are all you need to succeed. In the wrong hands, they can become weapons with which you can tear down others. In the right hands, they are a salve for the boredom, frustration and pain around you.

If you are lonely or depressed, if your wife or your husband has left you, if you are broke or greedy, if you are hungry for success or sick of your ambitions, if you are on a creative high or stuck in rut, if you know who you are or if you've outgrown your ambitions, whoever you want to be, *you must write.*

Writing is hard. Every writer will tell you there's a battle waging between us and a finished work.

Steven Pressfield, author of the *War of Art*, explains we writers have to slay our demons or dragons on the page.

"We're facing dragons too," he writes. "Fire-breathing griffins of the soul, whom we must outfight and outwit to reach the treasure of our self-in-potential to release the maiden who is God's plan and destiny for ourselves and the answer to why we were put on this planet."

Go now from this book and sit in a quiet room and face your dragons. Put one word after another on the blank page. Your sentences will make you feel sick. The awfulness of their construction will wound you. Your head will spin, and you will look outside and wonder if there's a better way to spend your time. Then when you're ready to quit, a great thing will happen.

You will write one true sentence.

This is how you will create something meaningful. This is how you will reinvent yourself. This is how you will leave a mark on your world, however small.

I apologise because I deceived you.

This book isn't a guide for more creative or productive writing. This book is my *Manifesto for Writing*.

What's yours?

THE END IS NEAR

Now that we've reached the end of *A Handbook For The Productive Writer*, I need your help. I need you to share some of your expert knowledge with me so I can improve my work.

If you have any suggestions for improving this book, if you have tips that I missed, please contact me by emailing bryan@ becomeawritertoday.com.

The beauty of self-publishing is it's easier than ever to update books with fresh and even more useful ideas. I can't promise I'll include everything in the next version of my book, but I will consider what you have to say.

Together, we can become better writers.

Don't forget to join my insider mailing list by visiting becomeawritertoday.com/join.

There, you can find out why I'm obsessed with the written word. You'll also receive lots of insider articles and an email course that will help you write faster.

GET THE POWER OF CREATIVITY SERIES

Book 1: Learning How to Build Lasting Habits,
Face Your Fears and Change Your Life

Book 2: An Uncommon Guide to Mastering Your
Inner Genius and Finding New Ideas That Matter

Book 3: How to Conquer Procrastination,
Finish Your Work and Find Success

www.thepowerofcreativitybook.com

ABOUT THE AUTHOR

IN THIS LIFE, Bryan Collins is an author.

In another life, he worked as a journalist and a radio producer. Before that, he plucked chickens. He is passionate about helping people accomplish more with their writing projects and when he's not writing, he's running.

Bryan makes his online home at www.becomeawritertoday.com. There, he writes about writing, creativity and productivity. His work has appeared on *Fast Company*, *Lifehacker* and *Copyblogger*.

Bryan holds a degree in communications and journalism, a diploma in social care, a masters degree in disability studies and a diploma in digital media.

You can reach him on Twitter @BryanJCollins, email bryan@becomeawritertoday.com or join his Facebook page Become a Writer Today.

Bryan is also the author of a three-part series: *The Power of Creativity* and the novella *Poor Brother, Rich Brother*.

He lives an hour outside of Dublin.

@bryanjcollins

Becomeawritertoday

www.becomeawritertoday.com

bryan@becomeawritertoday.com

AN ASK

I wrote, published and marketed *A Handbook for the Productive Writer*.

I'm passionate about what I do and about our craft. So, if you enjoyed this book or found it helpful in any way, please take a moment to **write a short review of my book** on <u>Goodreads</u>[4] or <u>Amazon</u>[5].

Your reviews mean more people will find and buy my book. Your reviews also mean I can write more books like this one.

Thank you for spending time reading my work.

---

4   https://www.goodreads.com/book/show/23545843-a-handbook-for-the-productive-writer

5   https://www.amazon.com/Handbook-Productive-Writer-Finish-Started-ebook/dp/B00MZEZIZ6

REFERENCES

Books

Altucher, James. *Choose Yourself*. 2013.

Allen, David. *Getting Things Done*. 2011.

Austen, Jane. *Pride and Prejudice*. 1992.

Babauta, Leo. *The Power of Less*. 2009.

Brown, Christy. *Down All the Days*. 1990.

Brown, Christy. *My Left Foot*. 1990.

Carnegie, Dale. *How to Win Friends and Influence People*. 1998.

Cheever, John. *The Journals*. 2011.

Covey, Stephen R. *The Seven Habits of Highly Effective People*. 2013.

Currey, Mason. *Daily Rituals: How Artists Work*. 2013.

Dickens, Charles. *A Tale of Two Cities*. 2011.

Doyle, Roddy. *The Commitments*. 2010

Doyle, Roddy. *The Snapper*. 2008.

Fitzgerald, Scott F. *The Great Gatsby*. 2013.

Franzen, Jonathan. *The Corrections*. 2010.

Gelb, Michael J. *How to Think Like Leonardo da Vinci*. 2000.

Isaacson, Walter. *Einstein: His Life and Universe*. 2008.

Isaacson, Walter. Steve Jobs: *The Exclusive Biography*. 2011.

Joyce, James. *Ulysses*. 2012.

Kafka, Franze. *Metamorphosis*. 2009.

Kennedy, Dan S. *The Ultimate Sales Letter: Attract New Customers and Boost Your Sales* (4th Ed). 2011.

King, Stephen. *On Writing Well: A Memoir of the Craft*. 2010.

Murakami, Haruki. *What I Talk About When I Talk About Running*. 2011.

Kleon, Austin. *Steal Like An Artist: 10 Things Nobody Told You About Being Creative*. 2012.

McKeown, Greg. *Essentialism: The Disciplined Pursuit of Less. 2014*

Levy, Mark. *Accidental Genius: Using Writing to Generate Your Best Ideas, Insight and Content* (Second Edition). 2009.

Nabokov, Vladimir. *Lolita*. 2012.

Pressfield, Steven and Coyne, Sean. *The War of Art*. 2011.

Plath, Sylvia. *The Bell Jar*. 2005.

McKee, Robert. *Story: Substance, Structure Style and The Principles of Screenwriting*. 1997.

Melville, Herman. *Moby Dick*. 2014.

Orwell, George. *1984*. 2013.

Platt, Sean. Truant, Johnny B. Wright, David. *Write. Publish. Repeat. The No Luck Required Guide to Self-Publishing Success*. 2013.

Salinger, J.D. *The Catcher in the Rye*. 2014.

Suzuki, Shunryu. Zen Mind, Beginner's Mind. 2011.

Tolstoy, Leo. *Anna Karenina*. 2012.

Vaynerchuk, Gary. *The Thank You Economy*. 2011.

Woolf, Virginia. *A Writer's Diary (1918-1941)*. 2013.

Zinsser, William. *On Writing Well*. 2006.

Articles and Online Resources

80Pct Solutions. *Freedom.* 2014. https://macfreedom.com/

Altucher, James. *The James Altucher Podcast: Episode 17: Chris Brogan: Are You a Freak?* by James Altucher (2014).

Björk, Johanna. *Benjamin Franklin's Routine: Do Good Each Day.* 2013. Taken from http://www.goodlifer.com/2013/02/benjamin-franklins-routine-do-good-each-day/ on July 4, 2014.

Burrell, Diana. Renegade Writer Q&A David Allen. Taken from http://www.therenegadewriter.com/2007/03/19/renegade-writer-qa-david-allen/ on June 24, 2014. Renegade Writer.

Chrisafis, Angelique.*Overlong, overrated and unmoving: Roddy Doyle's verdict on James Joyce's Ulysses.* 2004. Take from http://www.theguardian.com/uk/2004/feb/10/booksnews.ireland on June 21, 2014. The Guardian.

Colzato, Lorenza S. Ozturk, Ayca. Hommel, Bernhard. ˋ*Meditate to create: the impact of focused-attention and open-monitoring training on convergent and divergent thinking.* 2012. Taken from http://journal.frontiersin.org/Journal/10.3389/fpsyg.2012.00116/full on July 2, 2014. Leiden University.

Conradt, Stacy. *Vladamir Nabokov Talks Synesthesia* (2013). Taken from http://mentalfloss.com/article/49442/vladimir-nabokov-talks-synesthesia on June 21, 2014. Mental Floss.

David Foster Wallace on Ambition by blank on blank. Interview by Leonard Lopate, WNYC (1996). Taken from https://www.youtube.com/watch?v=w5R8gduPZw4 on June 24, 2014.

Devey, Joseph. *Sir Francis Bacon, The Advancement of Learning.* 2014. Taken from http://oll.libertyfund.org/titles/1433 on June 21, 2014. Online Library of Liberty.

Godin, Seth. The platform vs. the eyeballs. 2009. Taken from http://sethgodin.typepad.com/seths_blog/2009/09/the-platform-vs-the-eyeballs.html on June 21, 2014.

Gudgel, Andrew. *Commonplace Books – Old Wine in New Bottles.* 2010. Taken from http://www.andrewgudgel.com/commonplace.htm on June 21, 2014.

Guildhall, Olivia. *The Science of Why We Live*. Daily Telegraph. 2014.

Gilbert, Elizabeth: *Your Elusive Creative Genius*. 2009. Taken from http://www.ted.com/talks/elizabeth_gilbert_on_genius on June 21, 2014. TED.

Gray Matter. *Brain, Interrupted*. 2013. Taken from http://www.nytimes.com/2013/05/05/opinion/sunday/a-focus-on-distraction.html?r=1& on June 24, 2014. New York Times.

Hamilton, Jon. *Think You're Multitasking? Think Again*. 2008. Taken from http://www.npr.org/templates/story/story.php?storyId=95256794 on June 24, 2014. NPR.

Holiday, Ryan. *How and Why To Keep a Commonplace Book*. 2014. Taken from www.ryanholiday.net on June 21, 2014.

Isaac, Brad. *Jerry Seinfeld's Productivity Secret*. 2007. Taken from http://lifehacker.com/281626/jerry-seinfelds-productivity-secret on June 21, 2014. Lifehacker.

Lavinsky, Dane. *Pareto Principle: How To Use It to Dramatically Grow Your Business* by Dane Lavinsky, Forbes (2014). Taken from http://www.forbes.com/sites/davelavinsky/2014/01/20/pareto-principle-how-to-use-it-to-dramatically-grow-your-business/ on June 21, 2014. Forbes.

Lev Grossman. *Jonathan Franzen: Great American Novelist* by Lev Grossman. Time Magazine. 2010. Taken from http://content.time.com/time/magazine/article/0,9171,2010185,00.html on June 21, 2014. Time Magazine.

Mehta, Ravi. Zhu, Rui (Juliet) Zhu. Cheema, Amar. *Is Noise Always Bad? Exploring the Effects of Ambient Noise on Creative Cognition*. 2012. Taken from http://www.jstor.org/stable/10.1086/665048 on June 21, 2014. Chicago Journals.

Nielsen, Jakob. *How long do web users stay on webpages*. 2011 Take from http://www.nngroup.com/articles/how-long-do-users-stay-on-web-pages/ on June 21, 2014.

Plimpton, George. *Ernest Hemingway: The Art of Fiction No. 20*. 1954. Take from http://www.theparisreview.org/interviews/4825/the-art-of-fiction-no-21-ernest-hemingway on June 21, 2014. The Paris Review.

Side Dish *What Was Benjamin Franklin's Daily Routine?*. 2013. Take from http://www.sidedishmag.com/2013/07/me-and-benjamin.html on August 14, 2014. Side Dish.

The Air Force Departmental Publishing Office. *The Inverted Pyramid*. Taken from http://commons.wikimedia.org/wiki/File:Inverted_pyramid_2.svg#mediaviewer/File:Inverted_pyramid_2.svg on June 21, 2014.

Watts, Robert. *J.K. Rowling Unmasked As Author of Acclaimed Detective Novel* by Robert Watts. 2013. Taken from http://www.telegraph.co.uk/culture/books/10178344/JK-Rowling-unmasked-as-author-of-acclaimed-detective-novel.html on June 21, 2014. The Telegraph.

Viatour, Luc. *Vitruvian man*. 2014. Taken from www.Lucnix.be on June 21, 2014.

Writer's Relief Staff. *Famous Author Rejection Letters: True Stories Of Unbelievable Rejections*. 2011. Taken from http://writersrelief.com/blog/2011/07/famous-author-rejection-letters/ on July 3, 2014. Writer's Relief.